# CHECK YOUR VOCABULARY FOR

# ENGLISH FOR ACADEMIC PURPOSES

## A WORKBOOK FOR USERS

by

David Porter

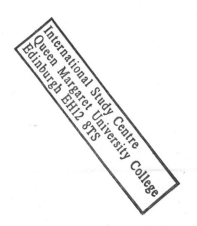

International Study Centre
Queen Margaret University College
Edinburgh EH12 8TS

Peter Collin Publishing

First published in Great Britain 2001

Published by Peter Collin Publishing Ltd
32-34 Great Peter Street, London, SW1P 2DB

© Peter Collin Publishing Ltd 2001

You may photocopy the inside pages of this workbook for classroom use only and not for resale
You are not licensed to copy the cover
All rights reserved

British Library Cataloguing in Publication Data
A catalogue entry for this book is available from the British Library

ISBN: 1-901659-53-4

Text typeset by The Studio Publishing Services, Exeter EX4 8JN
Printed by Nuffield Press, Abingdon

To Ana Rita

**Workbook Series**

*Check your:*

| | |
|---|---|
| Vocabulary for Academic Purposes | 1-901659-53-4 |
| Vocabulary for Banking and Finance | 0-948549-96-3 |
| Vocabulary for Business | 0-948549-72-6 |
| Vocabulary for Colloquial English | 0-948549-97-1 |
| Vocabulary for Computing | 0-948549-58-0 |
| Vocabulary for English: IELTS | 1-901659-60-7 |
| Vocabulary for English: FCE | 1-901659-11-9 |
| Vocabulary for English: TOEFL | 1-901659-68-2 |
| Vocabulary for Hotels, Tourism, Catering | 0-948549-75-0 |
| Vocabulary for Law | 1-901659-21-6 |
| Vocabulary for Marketing | 1-901659-48-8 |
| Vocabulary for Medicine | 0-948549-59-9 |

**English Dictionaries**

| | |
|---|---|
| English Dictionary for Students | 1-901659-06-2 |
| English Study Dictionary | 1-901659-63-1 |
| Dictionary of Accounting | 0-948549-27-0 |
| Dictionary of Agriculture, 2nd edition | 0-948549-78-5 |
| Dictionary of American Business | 0-948549-11-4 |
| Dictionary of Automobile Engineering | 0-948549-66-1 |
| Dictionary of Banking & Finance | 0-948549-12-2 |
| Dictionary of Business, 3rd edition | 1-901659-50-X |
| Dictionary of Computing, 3rd edition | 1-901659-04-6 |
| Dictionary of Ecology & Environment, 4th edition | 1-901659-61-5 |
| Dictionary of Government & Politics, 2nd edition | 0-948549-89-0 |
| Dictionary of Hotels, Tourism, Catering | 0-948549-40-8 |
| Dictionary of Human Resources, 2nd edition | 0-948549-79-3 |
| Dictionary of Information Technology, 3rd edition | 1-901659-55-0 |
| Dictionary of Law, 3rd edition | 1-901659-43-7 |
| Dictionary of Library & Information Management | 0-948549-68-8 |
| Dictionary of Marketing, 2nd edition | 0-948549-73-4 |
| Dictionary of Medicine, 3rd edition | 1-901659-45-3 |
| Dictionary of Printing & Publishing, 2nd edition | 0-948549-99-8 |

For details about our range of English and bilingual dictionaries and workbooks, please contact:

**Peter Collin Publishing**
32-34 Great Peter Street, London, SW1P 2DB
tel: +44 20 7222 1155    fax: +44 20 7222 1551
email: info@petercollin.com    website: **www.petercollin.com**

© Peter Collin Publishing 2001. For reference see *English Dictionary for Students* (1-901659-06-2)

# Contents

© Peter Collin Publishing 2001. For reference see *English Dictionary for Students* (1-901659-06-2)

# Introduction

The purpose of this book is to help students learn a common core of vocabulary which will be useful for almost any subject studied at college or university.

## Advice to the Student

### Obtain a Dictionary
Before attempting to use this book, you will need to obtain a good English-English dictionary, such as the *English Dictionary for Students* (ISBN: 1-901659-06-2) published by Peter Collin Publishing, which this workbook has been based on.

### Using your Dictionary
A dictionary is really a long list of individual words, but in normal situations, words are very rarely used on their own, appearing instead together with other words. For this reason, the vocabulary you will learn in this book is presented in example sentences which will help you to **understand** the words, to **remember** them more easily, and to **use** them correctly.

### Doing the Exercises
There are different types of exercises in this book, but one small example will be enough to show you how to use the book. In these two sentences from Unit One, notice first of all that the other words in these sentences show you the grammar of these words — here an adjective and then a verb.

1. Although not exactly identical, the two books are so _____ to each other that one writer must have copied much of his book from the other.

2. The Prime Minister set up a committee of financial experts to help him discuss and _____ new policies.

### Working Out the Word or Meaning
Also, notice that the other words in the sentences can help you to guess the meaning of the missing words. In the examples above, we can see from the phrases *not exactly identical* and *copied much of his book* that the adjective in the first example must mean something like *almost the same*. In the same way, because the *policies* mentioned in the second example are described as *new*, the verb in the second example seems to mean *plan* or *prepare*:

1. Although **not exactly identical**, the two books are so ___?_ adj _?___ to each other that one writer must have **copied much of his book** from the other.

2. The Prime Minister set up a committee of financial experts to help him discuss and ___?_ v _?___ **new** policies.

### Sample Answers
With the exercise from which these sentences were taken, the words *similar (adj)* and *formulate (v),* were included in the list of answers. Because of the grammar of these words and their meanings — which we can check in the dictionary if necessary — the completed sentences will look like this:

1. Although not exactly identical, the two books are so **similar** to each other that one writer must have copied much of his book from the other.

2. The Prime Minister set up a committee of financial experts to help him discuss and **formulate** new policies.

### Keep Your Own Notes
Next, whenever you find out what a new word means, write it into your vocabulary notebook, which you can organise in alphabetical order like a dictionary. With any new word, you should copy either the sentence from this book or the example from the dictionary. This will help you to learn the word.

© Peter Collin Publishing 2001. For reference see *English Dictionary for Students* (1-901659-06-2)

## Words With Many Meanings
When you do look in your dictionary, you may find that one word has many meanings. If you compare these, however, you will often find that they are not so different from each other, so try to look for one central meaning.

## Words That Go Together
Remember also to write down any other words which are often found together with your new word. For example, notice in your dictionary that we normally use the word *to* after the word *similar* (a dependent preposition) and that it is usually *policies, plans* or *programs* and so on which are *formulated* (examples of collocations). This information will help you to use the new words correctly.

## To sum up:
- decide if the word in the example sentence is a verb, a noun or an adjective
- read the other words to help you guess the meaning of the new word
- then if necessary use your dictionary to select a suitable answer
- if possible, choose one central meaning for the word from the dictionary entry
- write down your new word with an example sentence to help you remember its meaning
- note down any dependent prepositions or collocations to help you use the word correctly

# Advice to the Teacher

The purpose of this book is to equip non-native speakers of English at upper intermediate level and above with a core of sub-technical vocabulary relevant to the full range of university subjects.

It is envisaged that this book will be used to supplement an English for Academic Purposes/Study Skills course, at foundation, undergraduate or postgraduate level. It may either be used in class or be assigned for study on a self-access basis.

The vocabulary items presented here are based on research by I. S. P. Nation*, which culminated in a series of approximately 800 words ranked in sets according to their frequency of occurrence in texts drawn from a number of very different academic subjects.

Since the order of the eleven units presented in this book reflect this ranking, the words in Unit One have a wider range of application than those in Unit Two and so on, which means that students should work through the book sequentially.

Inside the units, each word is presented in an example sentence which aims firstly to provide a context from which students may be able to infer the meaning of the word in question and secondly to give instances of associated words such as collocates and dependent prepositions. This form of presentation will allow students to find out not only what words mean, but also how to use them.

The exercises include gap-filling, word matching, identifying synonyms, matching sentence fragments, and word-completion. In all cases, the style and content of the examples I have written are intended to be typical of language used in academic contexts.

In approaching the exercises, it is vital that students use dictionaries appropriately, and far preferable that they use a English-English learners dictionary rather than a translation dictionary. Similarly, it is important that students do not regard simply filling in blanks as the sole purpose of this book. Instead, students should approach vocabulary learning actively. This means keeping a vocabulary notebook in which they should be encouraged to write an example for each new word, with special attention being paid to any dependent prepositions and collocations.

Although the immediate goal is for students to learn the words here, if it can encourage students to take a more active, thoughtful approach to vocabulary learning, this book will have succeeded in its wider aim.

*Nation, I. S. P. (1990.) *Teaching and Learning Vocabulary*. Boston, MA: Heinle & Heinle.

© Peter Collin Publishing 2001. For reference see *English Dictionary for Students* (1-901659-06-2)

# Unit One

## 1a - Fill in the gaps

From the following list, use each word only once to complete the sentences below. Remember that in the case of nouns and verbs you may need to change the form of the word:

---

arbitrary (adj) • assign (v) • context (n) • criterion (n) • data (n)

denote (v) • devise (v) • usage (n) • ignore (v) • impact (n)

similar (adj) • summary (n) • formulate (v) • vertical (adj)

---

1. Although not exactly identical, the two books are so _____ to each other that one author must have copied much of his book from the other.

2. The Prime Minister set up a committee of financial experts to help him discuss and _____ new policies.

3. It is often possible to guess the meaning of a word from the other words around it — that is to say, the _____ .

4. About 100 years ago, Marconi _____ a way of using radio waves for communication.

5. In newspapers, the layout of the columns is _____ , while the rows run across the page horizontally.

6. The rise in the number of deaths from AIDS has had a very significant _____ on peoples sexual behaviour.

7. The _____ of drugs has increased significantly in spite of more severe penalties such as longer prison sentences.

8. Students should not try to write down everything they hear in a lecture, but just make a _____ of the most important points.

9. We use the term "class" to _____ groups of people who share the same social and economic backgrounds.

10. In one case, a murderer may go to prison for life, while another may be set free: it all seems completely _____ .

11. The new journalist was _____ to researching the election promises of the main political parties.

12. Before we can judge a government's success, we have to decide the _____ , such as unemployment, defence or taxation.

13. One student failed because he completely _____ the instructions on the paper, although they appeared at the top of every page.

14. Market researchers use _____ such as people's spending patterns as well as information about age and occupation to decide on the most effective marketing strategies.

---

*Don't forget to keep a record of the words and expressions that you have learnt, review your notes from time to time and try to use new vocabulary items whenever possible.*

© Peter Collin Publishing 2001. For reference see *English Dictionary for Students* (1-901659-06-2)

# 1b - Choose the right word

**In each of the sentences below, decide which word in *bold* is more suitable.**

1. During the 1970's and 1980's, it became increasingly *evident/visible* that companies in the West were uncompetitive.

2. The United Kingdom *makes/publishes* more books than any other country.

3. There has been a major road accident, *involving/including* 23 cars and 16 lorries.

4. On the basis of the latest survey, we know that most people have a very *negative/bleak* view of politicians and their parties.

5. In many parts of the world, people are becoming more worried about the danger of pollution and its effect on the *environment/ecology*.

6. Education experts from France travelled to Japan to *evaluate/judge* the secondary school system there.

7. Although it is not very big, the library has an excellent *range/variety* of books, journals and other resources for study.

8. Increasingly, the design of buildings is being *adjusted/modified* to allow easier access for disabled people.

9. The lack of extra student accommodation *restricted/narrowed* the expansion in student numbers which the university was planning.

10. Many students *acquire/derive* a great deal of enjoyment and satisfaction from their time at university.

11. Although the world is getting warmer slowly, the increase in temperature *varies/fluctuates* from country to country.

12. Following the bank raid, the police *followed/pursued* the robbers but were unable to catch them.

13. Assessment on this course *includes/consists* of coursework (30%) and examinations (70%).

> *Don't forget to keep a record of the words and expressions that you have learnt, review your notes from time to time and try to use new vocabulary items whenever possible.*

© Peter Collin Publishing 2001. For reference see *English Dictionary for Students* (1-901659-06-2)

# Unit One

## 1c - Finish the sentence

Choose the best ending for each of the sentence extracts below from the list underneath:

1. I like your essay, but I want you to **illustrate** ...
2. What will the result be if in the future we **assume** ...
3. Students may be asked to compare many **alternative** ...
4. The Channel Tunnel between France and England was **constructed** ...
5. Everyone wants to be happy, but we probably all **define** ...
6. Many universities now have language centres to **facilitate** ...
7. Numbers and results are not particularly useful in themselves; we need to **interpret** ...
8. In spite of warnings about cancer, many Westerners **equate** ...
9. Advertisers use a variety of **techniques** ...
10. At first, the police viewed the crimes as **random** ...
11. It may be the case that no solution is possible, given the **magnitude** ...
12. Although computers are becoming increasingly **complex**, ...
13. The investigation was stopped because the witnesses could not **identify** ...

a. ...theories, from which they have to select the most convincing.
b. ...happiness in many different ways.
c. ...that nearly everyone has access to a motor car?
d. ...the programs they use are becoming much easier to operate.
e. ...a sun tan with health and youthfulness.
f. ...the man they had seen commit the robbery.
g. ...language learning for international students.
h. ...at a cost of over £8 billion.
i. ...of this problem.
j. ...them to understand what they actually mean.
k. ...events, but realised later that there was a pattern linking them.
l. ...to persuade consumers to buy products and services.
m. ...your points by providing some supporting examples.

## 1d - Word substitution

From the list below, choose one word which could be used in place of the language shown in bold without changing the meaning of the sentence. Remember that you may need to change the form or in some cases the grammatical class of the word:

| | | | |
|---|---|---|---|
| comply with (v) | conclude (v) | equivalent (adj) | guarantee (n) |
| imply (v) | method (n) | obvious (adj) | presume (v) |
| proceed (v) | require (v) | specify (v) | sum (n) |

1. If a company does not **observe** health and safety laws, it may be fined very heavily if any of its workers are injured.  _____
2. For many years, $4 was **equal** to £1.  _____
3. University regulations **state** that students must pass 18 modules to graduate.  _____
4. Anybody driving a car **is obliged** by law to have insurance.  _____

© Peter Collin Publishing 2001. For reference see *English Dictionary for Students* (1-901659-06-2)

5. On the basis of their examination results, it was **clear** that most students had completely misunderstood the first part of the paper. _____

6. Many people think that oil will run out in the next 100 years, but they are **assuming** that we will continue to use oil at the same rate as today. _____

7. Most electrical products have a one- or two-year **warranty** in case something should go wrong. _____

8. One problem facing overseas students is adapting to new teaching **techniques**. _____

9. The fact that crime increases when unemployment goes up seems to **suggest** a link between the two. _____

10. It will cost an overseas student at least £10,000 per year to live and study in Britain, which is a very large **amount** of money. _____

11. The lecturer gave the students a 10 minute break before **continuing** with the rest of her lecture. _____

12. At the end of her talk, the lecturer **finished** with a brief review of the main points. _____

## 1e - Choose the best word

**For each of the following sentences, choose the best word from a, b or c.**

1. In this first assignment, we will _____ your work and then give you detailed feedback on how to improve your writing.
   *a. assess*        *b. judge*        *c. measure*

2. In a seminar or tutorial, everyone should take part rather than allow one person to _____ the discussion.
   *a. overwhelm*        *b. dominate*        *c. oppress*

3. Although it is impossible to give a _____ age, we believe that the woman was between 25 and 30 when she died.
   *a. definite*        *b. certain*        *c. absolute*

4. Rather than try to treat it, the best _____ to the problem of poor public health may be to attempt to prevent it.
   *a. way*        *b. method*        *c. approach*

5. Surprisingly perhaps, the biggest _____ health risk for tourists travelling abroad is actually road traffic accidents.
   *a. potential*        *b. possible*        *c. theoretical*

6. Water is made up of two _____ , namely oxygen and hydrogen.
   *a. sections*        *b. aspects*        *c. elements*

7. Computers can be difficult to repair because there may be hundreds of different _____ inside.
   *a. components*        *b. pieces*        *c. parts*

8. Because Paris is expensive, many organisations pay higher salaries to _____ for the high cost of living there.
   *a. compensate*        *b. adjust*        *c. redress*

9. Many people were killed instantly at Hiroshima and Nagasaki, but thousands more died from _____ radiation sickness.
   *a. succeeding*        *b. following*        *c. subsequent*

10. The clothing of men and women used to be quite _____ , whereas today women often wear trousers as well as men.
    *a. distinct*        *b. diverse*        *c. distinguished*

11. Research _____ that customers want free car-parking when they go shopping.
    *a. claims*        *b. indicates*        *c. points out*

12. In political terms, the Middle East is one of the most unstable _____ of the world.
    *a. locations*        *b. places*        *c. regions*

13. The _____ cause of death today in Britain is heart disease, with cancer in second place.
    *a. first*        *b. prime*        *c. initial*

© Peter Collin Publishing 2001. For reference see *English Dictionary for Students* (1-901659-06-2)

# Unit One

## 1f - Make a collocation

Start by reading through the sentences below. Then take one word from the box on the left and combine this with one from the box on the right to make a collocation. For example, *valid* can be joined with *reason*. (Note that more than one pairing may be possible and also that some words appear more than once.) Then try to match your combinations with the spaces in the sentences below:

| put forward • ultimate • establish<br>reverse • initial • analyse • new<br>valid • new • tense • leading<br>marital • minimum • constant | status • concept • responsibility • results<br>the verdict • role • atmosphere • reason<br>temperature • the hypothesis • a link<br>requirement • dimension • results |

1. If you submit work late, you will lose marks and may even be given a fail grade, unless you have a _____ _____ such as illness.

2. One travel company is now advertising a completely _____ _____ in tourism: flights into outer space by rocket.

3. At the bottom of the ocean, the water remains at a _____ _____ irrespective of changing weather conditions at the surface.

4. The growth of China will add a _____ _____ to the economic and political situation in the Far East.

5. Students are expected not just to describe what they have done but also to _____ _____ when they write a research report.

6. Investigators have been able to _____ _____ between childhood illnesses and industrial pollution.

7. Following the demonstrations by thousands of students, there was a very _____ _____ in the capital, with many choosing to leave the city and head for the countryside.

8. Unfortunately, although the _____ _____ were very promising, the project failed in the long run because of a lack of interest.

9. Engineers have played a _____ _____ in improving our health by giving us clean water supplies, perhaps more so than doctors.

10. The Managing Director may run the company, but _____ _____ rests with the Board of Directors.

11. On the form, please give your name, nationality, address and indicate your _____ _____ .

12. When some scientists originally _____ _____ known as global warming, the idea was not taken seriously, and yet today it is accepted by nearly everyone.

13. In some instances, a Court of Appeal may _____ _____ reached at the first trial and released somebody who has been wrongly held in prison.

14. Most universities require international students to have an IELTS score of 6 (equivalent to a TOEFL score of 550) as a _____ _____ for English language competence.

© Peter Collin Publishing 2001. For reference see *English Dictionary for Students* (1-901659-06-2)

## Vocabulary sheet

*Don't forget to keep a record of the words and expressions that you have learnt, review your notes from time to time and try to use new vocabulary items whenever possible.*

© Peter Collin Publishing 2001. For reference see *English Dictionary for Students* (1-901659-06-2)

# Unit Two

## 2a - Fill in the gaps

From the following list, use each word only once to complete the sentences below. Remember that in the case of nouns and verbs you may need to change the form of the word:

achieve (v) • automatic (adj) • conceive (v) • create (v) • ensue (v)

equilibrium (n) • manipulate (v) • mathematics (n) • innovative (adj)

period (n) • precede (v) • section (n) • series (n) • stable (adj) • tradition (n)

1. In order to be successful, some politicians _____ other people to get what they want.

2. Japanese and Korean companies have invested heavily in the UK, _____ thousands of new jobs.

3. The Internet was first _____ of as a way of linking computers in the USA together.

4. Serious unrest and rioting _____ as a result of the decision to ignore the result of the election.

5. Since consumers are always demanding new products, companies which can be _____ are more likely to succeed.

6. Most planes today are controlled not by human pilots but by a computer system known as an _____ pilot, which is even responsible for taking off and landing.

7. Most employers insist that their employees have qualifications in English and _____ .

8. Some academics have argued that standards have been falling because more students are _____ first class degrees.

9. Over a _____ of twenty years, the economy grew at an average of 8% per year.

10. The price of a product will not change if there is _____ between the supply and the demand for that product.

11. By _____ , wedding guests in most cultures give presents or money to the newly-married couple.

12. In addition to the regular lectures, we have a _____ of public lectures given by guest speakers from other universities.

13. Although the arrival of coffee in Britain _____ that of tea, it is the second drink which is the more popular today.

14. Reports are usually divided into separate _____ with headings such as 'Findings' and 'Conclusions.'

15. After a very difficult night, his blood pressure became _____ again and his family were allowed to visit him.

© Peter Collin Publishing 2001. For reference see *English Dictionary for Students* (1-901659-06-2)

## 2b - Choose the right word

**In each of the sentences below, decide which of the *bold* words is more suitable.**

1. A new moon *occurs/takes place* every 28 days.

2. Students should not be *inert/passive* but should try instead to contribute as much as possible to discussions in seminar groups.

3. On the first day, the course director and the subject tutor explained their *respective/single* roles to the new students.

4. It is now possible to *infer/imply* a link between using mobile phones and contracting some forms of cancer.

5. The fact that population growth is still *accelerating/catching up* is one of the most important problems we face.

6. Most universities need to earn money from private sources, but the *important/major* part of their funding still comes from the government.

7. Expenditure on weapons such as guns, tanks and aeroplanes consumes a large *piece/portion* of a country's wealth.

8. Because foreign exchange rates *ebb and flow/fluctuate*, it is not always possible for exporters to know how much money they will receive from sales.

9. Member countries *award/contribute* money to the United Nations to pay for the running of the organisation.

10. The main *concentration/focus* of Greenpeace is on problems concerning pollution.

11. Although their *plan/design* was often very good, the quality of many British cars tended to be poor.

12. Although it is very expensive, it is possible to *convert/exchange* other forms of carbon into diamonds.

13. Prehistoric man could not *think/comprehend* why the moon appears to grow bigger and then smaller each month.

14. In some situations, a law court can *authorise/let* the police to enter a house without the owner's permission.

> *Don't forget to keep a record of the words and expressions that you have learnt, review your notes from time to time and try to use new vocabulary items whenever possible.*

© Peter Collin Publishing 2001. For reference see *English Dictionary for Students* (1-901659-06-2)

# Unit Two

## 2c - Finish the sentence

Choose the best ending for each of the sentence extracts below from the list underneath:

1. In 1905, Einstein published the first part of his **theory**...

2. Environmentalists point out that electric cars just **shift**...

3. Most metals **expand**...

4. As a result of the **intense**...

5. Fifty years ago, most smokers were not **aware**...

6. The new grading machine has the **function**...

7. In many universities, there is a coffee bar **adjacent**...

8. After studying for two hours, it becomes difficult to **concentrate**...

9. Some children show a great deal of **maturity**...

10. Sadly, according to government **statistics,** ...

11. In the seventeenth century, Galileo **demonstrated**...

12. In the 1980's, the US and Soviet governments made the **crucial**...

13. Politicians often complain that newspapers **distort**...

14. The history of the Americas is usually from seen from the **perspective**...

15. An already difficult operation was **complicated**...

---

a. ...of the dangers of smoking.

b. ...at a young age, while others may continue to be irresponsible.

c. ...to the library where students can take a break.

d. ...the pollution problem from the car itself to the electricity station.

e. ...that all objects (heavy or light) fall at the same speed.

f. ...heat of the fire, the front half of the train was completely destroyed

g. ...what they say so that the readers cannot read the truth.

h. ...of relativity, which completely changed our ideas of time and space.

i. ...of the European immigrants, rather than from that of the original inhabitants.

j. ...on your work and so it is a good idea to take a break.

k. ...when they are heated.

l. ...of separating the larger pieces of metal from the smaller pieces.

m. ...over 30% of marriages end in divorce within five years.

n. ...decision to reduce the number of atomic weapons.

o. ...by the fact that the patient had a history of heart disease.

© Peter Collin Publishing 2001. For reference see *English Dictionary for Students* (1-901659-06-2)

## 2d - Word substitution

From the list below, choose one word which could be used in place of the language shown in *bold* without changing the meaning of the sentence. Remember that you may need to change the form or in some cases the grammatical class of the word:

> affect (v) • capillary (n) • notion (n) • decade (n) • emphasize (v)
>
> expose (v) • generate (v) • consequent (adj) • pertinent (adj)
>
> predict (v) • select (v) • signify (v) • structure (n) • undergo (v)

1. Over the previous **ten years**, we have seen an enormous growth in the number of home personal computers.

2. Lecturers often speak more loudly and more slowly when they want to **stress** an important point.

3. One important function of newspapers is to **uncover** dishonest behaviour and wrong-doing by those in power.

4. The **organisation** of the company has changed completely, with far fewer senior managers.

5. The decision to give longer prison sentences **indicated** a hardening of the governments attitude towards drug offenders.

6. The new computer system **created** a lot of interest among potential customers.

7. When the government increased the tax on petrol, there was a **resultant** rise in transport costs.

8. In the first instance, the blood passes out of the heart, through the lungs and along the arteries before reaching the **small blood vessels** within the skin.

9. Until the sixteenth century, the idea that the Earth moves around the Sun was regarded as a ridiculous idea, whereas today we accept this **concept** as completely normal.

10. Pollution is a problem which has an **effect** on every country today.

11. Most economists **forecast** that China will become a leading world economy in the twenty-first century.

12. One difficult aspect of writing an essay is selecting material which is **relevant** to the topic and excluding irrelevant information.

13. The company has **experienced** a number of significant changes in the last few years.

14. The first thing to do is to **choose** the courses which you would like to study and then look at each university prospectus.

> *Don't forget to keep a record of the words and expressions that you have learnt, review your notes from time to time and try to use new vocabulary items whenever possible.*

© Peter Collin Publishing 2001. For reference see *English Dictionary for Students* (1-901659-06-2)

# Unit Two

## 2e - Choose the best word

For each of the following sentences, choose the best word from *a, b or c*.

1. Although he had no _____ injuries, doctors later found that he was suffering from internal bleeding.
   a. outside            b. external            c. outlying

2. There is a marked _____ between the poverty of the poorest members of society and the affluence of the richest.
   a. opposite           b. contrast            c. variation

3. The allied forces launched _____ bombing raids on several important sites in and around the enemy capital.
   a. simultaneous       b. contemporary        c. coincidental

4. Students are often advised to look at the first and last _____ of a book before attempting to read it in detail.
   a. headings           b. chapters            c. titles

5. Although this is far from certain, the _____ age of the universe is about 4.6 billion years.
   a. approximate        b. general             c. rough

6. Some economists argue that new _____ causes unemployment while others feel that it allows more jobs to be created.
   a. science            b. engineering         c. technology

7. After you have submitted your application, the university will attempt to _____ that the information you have supplied is correct.
   a. verify             b. certify             c. investigate

8. Young children go through a _____ in their development when they try to copy everything they hear.
   a. process            b. phase               c. transition

9. In some countries, there is no tax on books on the _____ that education should not be taxed.
   a. principle          b. idea                c. concept

10. Further information can be _____ from the nearest British Council office.
    a. obtained          b. found               c. got

11. As everyone knows, certain metals such as iron and steel can have a _____ field while others like copper cannot.
    a. electrical        b. magnetic            c. chemical

12. Just as dividing up an orange into _____ makes it easier to eat, always try to break up a longer piece of text into small blocks of words.
    a. segments          b. pieces              c. sections

13. One problem for any teacher is that each student has his/her own _____ needs.
    a. separate          b. individual          c. distinctive

14. Good theories are important of course, but we must have _____ evidence to support them.
    a. empirical         b. true                c. realistic

© Peter Collin Publishing 2001. For reference see *English Dictionary for Students* (1-901659-06-2)

## 2f - Make a collocation

**Start by reading through the sentences below. Then take one word from the box on the left and combine this with one from the box on the right to make a collocation. (Note that more than one pairing may be possible and also that some words appear more than once.) Then try to match your combinations with the spaces in the sentences below:**

| |
|---|
| endangered • devote • assert reacted • precise • sequence of highly • inhibit • verbal • separate transmit • economically • natural |

| |
|---|
| events • signals • details • entities time and money • sophisticated species • agreement • phenomena angrily • feasible • the right • growth |

1. In spite of advances in technology, we are still at risk from _____ _____ such as earthquakes and floods.

2. One threat facing companies today is _____ _____ computer 'hackers' who break into the most advanced computer systems.

3. The accident was the result of a tragic _____ _____ which could have been prevented with better safety procedures.

4. The company _____ _____ to the suggestion that its products were unsafe.

5. Although it would be expensive, some American scientists think that a manned trip to Mars is technically and _____ _____

6. Tigers (and other large cats) are now an _____ _____ and may disappear altogether in the future.

7. After the Second World War, African nations started to _____ _____ to become independent.

8. In law, a _____ _____ even though it is not written down like a formal contract, is still a contract.

9. While she refused to give any _____ _____ , the Minister admitted that several people had been arrested.

10. In order to produce new medicines, drug companies have to _____ _____ on a huge scale to their research and development activities.

11. Most economists believe that high taxes _____ _____ in the economy.

12. In spite of its age, the satellite is still continuing to _____ _____ to Earth.

13. Are the mind and body the same thing or are they two _____ _____ ?

© Peter Collin Publishing 2001. For reference see *English Dictionary for Students* (1-901659-06-2)

# Unit Two

## Vocabulary sheet

_____

_____

_____

_____

_____

_____

_____

_____

_____

_____

_____

_____

_____

_____

_____

_____

_____

_____

_____

_____

_____

_____

_____

_____

_____

_____

_____

Unit Two

> _Don't forget to keep a record of the words and expressions that you have learnt, review your notes from time to time and try to use new vocabulary items whenever possible._

© Peter Collin Publishing 2001. For reference see _English Dictionary for Students_ (1-901659-06-2)

## 3a - Fill in the gaps

**From the following list, use each word only once to complete the sentences below. Remember that in the case of nouns and verbs you may need to change the form of the word:**

---

co-ordinate (v) • discrete (adj) • estimate (n) • geography (n)

norm (n) • pole (n) • preposition (n) • rational (adj)

scheme (n) • source (n) • task (n) • underlie (v)

---

1. Paying for large purchases by credit card instead of in cash has become the _____ in many parts of the world.

2. Although speech is mostly continuous sound, written language is divided up into _____ units which we call words.

3. One of the roles of the Managing Director is to _____ the work of different departments to ensure that they work well together.

4. In _____ , we study the physical features of the world — such as rivers and mountains — and how we make use of them.

5. The purpose of a bibliography at the end of an essay is to show the _____ of information used in writing the essay.

6. Remember that some verbs may need to be followed by a _____ , such as lead to, result in, and so on.

7. Although we cannot be sure, most _____ point to an increase in average air temperatures of about 2.0°C in the next 100 years.

8. Everyone knows that diseases such as malaria are on the increase again, but what we are not so sure about is the _____ cause of this.

9. Most economic theories assume that people act on a _____ basis, but this doesn't take account of the fact that we often use our emotions instead.

10. Most countries in the Far East have developed very quickly, while at the opposite _____ many Third World countries have not grown at all.

11. The government has launched a new _____ aimed at reducing youth unemployment.

12. While half of the students were responsible for writing the questionnaires, the others had the _____ of analysing the data.

---

*Don't forget to keep a record of the words and expressions that you have learnt, review your notes from time to time and try to use new vocabulary items whenever possible.*

© Peter Collin Publishing 2001. For reference see *English Dictionary for Students* (1-901659-06-2)

# Unit Three

## 3b - Choose the right word

In each of the sentences below, decide which of the words in *bold* is more suitable.

1. If somebody has a diet which is *deficient/inadequate* in vitamins, he/she may suffer poor health as a result.

2. Although the characters were very convincing, the *tale/plot* was so weak that the film was a failure.

3. The *transition/transit* from a communist to a free-market economy has been very difficult for a number of countries.

4. Students usually dress casually at university, but this style of dress is not *correct/appropriate* when they start work.

5. The opinions expressed in a newspaper usually reflect the views of the *proprietor/landlord.*

6. In the USA and Japan, extreme religious groups living in isolated *communes/societies* have been responsible for a number of violent crimes.

7. In order to discuss the implications of the crisis, the President *convened/gathered* a meeting of his top advisors at the White House.

8. Because of the growth in the number of communication *stations/satellites* in space, viewers have access to more television channels.

9. An important social and political *topic/issue* in many developed countries is the growing number of old people.

10. Sometimes, unexpected economic changes force an organisation to *deviate/divert* from its original business plan.

11. There are many reasons behind the success of the fastest-growing economies, but one common *factor/idea* seems to be high levels of education.

12. Because the weather was so bad, the astronauts *abandoned/left* their attempt to launch the space shuttle.

---

> *Don't forget to keep a record of the words and expressions that you have learnt, review your notes from time to time and try to use new vocabulary items whenever possible.*

© Peter Collin Publishing 2001. For reference see *English Dictionary for Students* (1-901659-06-2)

## 3c - Finish the sentence

Choose the best ending for each of the sentence extracts below from the list underneath:

1. Resentment and jealousy over jobs is a common source of **conflict...**

2. Many members of the public question the **relevance**...

3. Retraining courses for the unemployed may just be a way to **exclude**...

4. The letters L, E and C on the map **correspond**...

5. Some environmentalists have a very bleak **vision**...

6. One way in which some countries can produce very cheap goods is to **exploit**...

7. The demonstrators refused to **disperse**,...

8. Multi-national companies are often keen to **seek**...

9. The Earth **rotates**...

10. It is better to work at a constant rate and to **maintain**...

11. Nowadays, most people have a more favourable **attitude**...

12. If a family moves abroad, the children often **adapt**...

---

a. ...to their new environment more quickly than their parents.

b. ...towards women having top positions in the workplace.

c. ...within society and can lead to violence.

d. ...to London, Edinburgh and Cardiff.

e. ...although the police were heavily armed and very aggressive.

f. ...more people from the unemployment totals.

g. ...child workers by paying them very low wages.

h. ...this during the year rather than to try to learn everything the night before the examinations.

i. ...on its axis once every 24 hours.

j. ...of the monarchy to life in modern society.

k. ...local companies in developing economies willing to act as partners.

l. ...of the future, while others are much more optimistic.

© Peter Collin Publishing 2001. For reference see *English Dictionary for Students* (1-901659-06-2)

# Unit Three

## 3d - Word substitution

From the list below, choose one word which could be used in place of the language shown in *bold* without changing the meaning of the sentence. Remember that you may need to change the form or in some cases the grammatical class of the word:

---

accomplish (v) • adequate (adj) • area (n) • chemical (n)

conduct (n) • consume (v) • credible (adj) • dispose of (v)

exert (v) • manifest in (v) • occupy (v) • rely on (v)

---

1. Environmentalists are keen to persuade us to **throw away** rubbish and waste in more environmentally-friendly ways.

2. Poisonous **substances** released into the sea may be absorbed by fish and then find their way into the human food chain.

3. A growing number of scientists find it **plausible** that other life forms may exist elsewhere in the universe.

4. Some countries have such great economic problems that they are forced to **depend on** aid from richer countries in order to feed their inhabitants.

5. Before accepting an overseas student, a university will make sure that the student's English is **sufficient**.

6. The North Americans **use** more energy and resources than any other nation.

7. Although Mozart lived for only 40 years, he **achieved** a great deal in his short life.

8. At examination time, go to the library early as all the places tend to be **filled** very quickly.

9. Because of its economic and military strength, the USA **exercises** considerable influence over world politics.

10. He suffers from a lack of self-confidence, as **shown by** his very poor examination results.

11. Prisoners are sometimes released from prison early if their **behaviour** has been good.

12. If global warming continues, many **regions** of the world will become drier while others may become wetter.

© Peter Collin Publishing 2001. For reference see *English Dictionary for Students* (1-901659-06-2)

# 3e - Choose the best word

For each of the following sentences, choose the best word from *a, b or c.*

1. Before giving a presentation, always _____ the focus on the projector so that everyone can read what is on the screen.

   *a. adjust*          *b. move*          *c. change*

2. The changes companies make to their cars are often very _____ and may not change the basic structure of the cars at all.

   *a. microscopic*          *b. superficial*          *c. minute*

3. Although most cars can travel much faster, the _____ speed limit in the UK is 70 mph (110 kph).

   *a. maximum*          *b. highest*          *c. biggest*

4. In special _____ , a person who is found guilty of murder may receive no punishment at all from the court.

   *a. places*          *b. times*          *c. circumstances*

5. The results of the government inquiry _____ that there had been no deliberate attempt by the company to deceive investors.

   *a. displayed*          *b. revealed*          *c. explained*

6. One important aspect of marketing is to create a positive _____ of a company or product.

   *a. image*          *b. picture*          *c. style*

7. Today, people are probably more familiar with _____ on the television and radio rather than in the theatre.

   *a. drama*          *b. acting*          *c. play*

8. Police could not understand why the arrested man had murdered his neighbour since he appeared to have no _____ .

   *a. objective*          *b. motive*          *c. purpose*

9. The first two weeks of the course are designed to _____ new students and to allow them to settle into university life.

   *a. orientate*          *b. instruct*          *c. introduce*

10. The instructions from air traffic control were not fully _____ , and as a result the pilot made an error and crashed.

    *a. total*          *b. explicit*          *c. complete*

11. A large number of people became ill after receiving blood transfusions _____ with the AIDS virus.

    *a. polluted*          *b. poisoned*          *c. contaminated*

12. Joining a newsgroup allows computer users to make _____ with other people who share a similar interest.

    *a. touch*          *b. approach*          *c. contact*

13. If you have time, I would really _____ some help with this assignment.

    *a. appreciate*          *b. respect*          *c. value*

© Peter Collin Publishing 2001. For reference see *English Dictionary for Students* (1-901659-06-2)

# Unit Three

## 3f - Make a collocation

**Start by reading through the sentences below. Then take one word from the box on the left and combine this with one from the box on the right to make a collocation. (Note that more than one pairing may be possible and also that some words appear more than once.) Then try to match your combinations with the spaces in the sentences below:**

| global • power and • outspoken |
|---|
| physical • common • previous |
| dynamic • labour • computer |
| final • positive • classic |

| shortage • prestige • experience |
|---|
| aspects • personality • example |
| decision • network • exercise |
| critic • feature • economy |

1.  After the Second World War, there was a _____ _____ in Britain and so workers from other countries had to be recruited.

2.  Some people found Mrs Thatcher's style somewhat aggressive, while others preferred to regard her as having a forceful and _____ _____ .

3.  His doctor advised him to give up fatty foods and to take some form of _____ _____ such as golf.

4.  In most countries, Mercedes-Benz cars are very famous because they are regarded as symbols of _____ _____ .

5.  The university refused to make a _____ _____ on his application until he had taken a language test.

6.  Without doubt, Coca-Cola is probably the _____ _____ of a product that is known world-wide.

7.  Employers are always keen to recruit staff with good qualifications and relevant _____ _____ .

8.  Those language learners who focus on the _____ _____ of living in a new culture rather than on the disadvantages tend to learn more quickly.

9.  Because she was an _____ _____ of the government, she was kept under house arrest for a number of years.

10. Unfortunately, rising crime rates seem to be an increasingly _____ _____ of life in big cities today.

11. The Internet, as the name implies, is really a huge _____ _____ , linking computers all over the world.

12. Tourism is now a very significant part of the _____ _____ , earning millions of dollars.

© Peter Collin Publishing 2001. For reference see *English Dictionary for Students* (1-901659-06-2)

## Vocabulary sheet

*Don't forget to keep a record of the words and expressions that you have learnt, review your notes from time to time and try to use new vocabulary items whenever possible.*

© Peter Collin Publishing 2001. For reference see *English Dictionary for Students* (1-901659-06-2)

# Unit Four

## 4a - Fill in the gaps

From the following list, use each word only once to complete the sentences below. Remember that in the case of nouns and verbs you may need to change the form of the word:

administer (v) • analogy (n) • assemble (v) • distribute (v)

energy (n) • impress (v) • intervene (v) • perpendicular (adj)

reject (v) • speculate (v) • spontaneous (adj) • text (n)

1. She so _____ the interviewers that they gave her the job.

2. At the beginning of the examination, question papers were _____ to all of the candidates in the hall.

3. Artificial intelligence draws an _____ between the digital computer and the human brain, but some researchers think that this comparison is too simplistic.

4. Studying a language can take up a great deal of time, money and _____ .

5. Following the earthquake, the house was unsafe because the walls were no longer _____ .

6. Although there is very little evidence, many scientists _____ that life may exist on other planets.

7. The spell-check facility on a computer allows students to check the _____ of their assignments for basic errors.

8. The police have a duty to _____ the law fairly and give everyone the same treatment.

9. For some university courses, the majority of applications are _____ because the competition for places is so great.

10. Usually, we try to reach a conclusion after careful thought, but sometimes we may make _____ decisions instead.

11. A large number of people _____ outside the Parliament to show support for their party.

12. Because hundreds of people were dying, the United Nations decided to _____ and provide emergency food supplies.

## 4b - Choose the right word

In each of the sentences below, decide which word in *bold* is more suitable.

1. Although he was interested in many fields, Einstein is best known for his work in the *sphere/globe* of physics.

2. *Psychology/Biology* can help the police understand how criminals think.

3. Following the explosion at Chernobyl, scientists were keen to *assess/investigate* the cause of the accident.

4. The imaginary line between the North Pole and the South Pole is known as the Earths *axis/axle*.

5. At the end of the year, the bank *praises/appraises* all of its staff and gives a bonus to the best performers.

© Peter Collin Publishing 2001. For reference see *English Dictionary for Students* (1-901659-06-2)

6. If you are taking notes in a lecture, use **shapes/symbols** such as + and = as opposed to the words and and equals.

7. The principle of **heredity/inheritance** explains why children tend to look like their parents.

8. The two sides have been engaged for some hours now in a lengthy **discourse/chat** on the issue of weapons, with no conclusions as yet.

9. After he had moved to Australia, he started to **acquire/obtain** a marked Australian accent.

10. Although the work is far from finished, some **approximate/tentative** conclusions can already be drawn from the responses we have so far.

11. In a dangerous situation, most people panic and become very frightened, while others show no **emotion/sympathy** at all.

## 4c - Finish the sentence

**Choose the best ending for each of the sentence extracts below from the list underneath:**

1. On the screen above me, you can see a **diagram**...

2. In mathematics, a statement is known as a **theorem**...

3. The student population is much more **diverse**...

4. Older university buildings may be wonderful in **aesthetic**...

5. The contract **stipulated**...

6. The Internet may soon not be **capable**...

7. The police usually contact parents about any **incident**...

8. Because of pollution in the **atmosphere,** ...

9. The terrorists demanded that the government **release**...

10. One journalist asked the minister to **justify**...

11. The negotiations went on through the night, but the **eventual**...

12. Heavy rains **persisted**...

a. ...terms, but are not always very practical.

b. ...more UV radiation is reaching the Earth, resulting in more skin cancer.

c. ...his decision to reduce spending on education.

d. ...showing the different parts of the system.

e. ...than in the past, with many more part-time and mature students.

f. ...which involves young children.

g. ...outcome was agreement on all the main points.

h. ...for several days, causing heavy flooding.

i. ...their colleagues from prison.

j. ...of sending all the information users want.

k. ...if we can prove it by using logic and reasoning.

l. ...that all the goods had to be delivered within four weeks.

25

# Unit Four

## 4d - Word substitution

From the list below, choose one word which could be used in place of the language shown in **bold** without changing the meaning of the sentence. Remember that you may need to change the form or in some cases the grammatical class of the word:

---

| | | | |
|---|---|---|---|
| allege (v) • | alter (v) • | cease (v) • | elaborate (adj) |
| fragment (n) • | philosophy (n) | • | litigation (n) |
| induce (v) • | reservoir (n) • | subside (v) • | upsurge (n) |

1.  The prisoner **claimed** that he had been attacked by the police, but there was no _____ evidence to prove this.

2.  Because of the possible link between disease in cows and humans, many _____ companies **stopped** trading in British beef and associated products.

3.  Your research proposal doesn't need to be too **detailed**: keep it simple and _____ concentrate on the main points.

4.  Global warming will **change** the way we live: everybody will experience some _____ change.

5.  Following an air accident, investigators examine every **piece** of the wreckage _____ to determine the cause of the crash.

6.  The most recent management **thinking** encourages managers to listen more _____ carefully to the ideas of their employees.

7.  During the last twenty-five years, there has been a significant **increase** in the _____ number of overseas students in British universities.

8.  When the interest in the company **declined**, the value of its shares began to _____ fall.

9.  The government's refusal to accept the result of the election **prompted** _____ thousands of people to come out on to the streets and protest.

10. As so many jobs require good skills, there is a **pool** of people who are _____ unemployed because they do not have any skills.

11. A number of universities are worried about **legal action** in the law courts by _____ students who are dissatisfied with their courses.

© Peter Collin Publishing 2001. For reference see *English Dictionary for Students* (1-901659-06-2)

## 4e - Choose the best word

**For each of the following sentences, choose the best word from *a, b* or *c*.**

1.  The former West Germany tried to _____ its business approach onto the former East Germany.

    *a. imprint*               *b. enforce*               *c. superimpose*

2.  In a nuclear power station, _____ of uranium are split into smaller particles, releasing huge amounts of energy.

    *a. atoms*                 *b. chunks*                *c. elements*

3.  Young army officers led the violent _____ which brought down the democratically-elected government.

    *a. revolt*                *b. policy*                *c. way*

4.  The recent rise in leukaemia and similar diseases has been _____ radiation leaking from the nearby nuclear power station.

    *a. credited to*           *b. led to*                *c. attributed to*

5.  One of the reasons for the relatively high price of many drugs is the huge cost of _____ and development.

    *a. experiments*           *b. research*              *c. trials*

6.  The Channel Tunnel between France and the United Kingdom was a huge engineering _____ .

    *a. project*               *b. development*           *c. attempt*

7.  We have two e-mail systems here: one for _____ use, and another for contacting people outside the university.

    *a. inside*                *b. internal*              *c. indoors*

8.  The police interviewed three men but later _____ them from their investigation as they were all innocent.

    *a. eliminated*            *b. eradicated*            *c. exterminated*

9.  A computer cannot guess the answer to a question, since all its operations are based on _____ .

    *a. logic*                 *b. thought*               *c. understanding*

10. The _____ of the American space programme in the 1960's was to put a man on the moon by the end of the decade.

    *a. ambition*              *b. point*                 *c. goal*

11. If public transport is to succeed in serving the public, it is important to _____ services such as trains and buses so that they work together and offer a more convenient service.

    *a. integrate*             *b. unite*                 *c. combine*

12. Approximately 30 of the world's most industrialised countries _____ the Organisation for Economic Cooperation and Development.

    *a. constitute*            *b. comprise*              *c. are composed of*

**27**

© Peter Collin Publishing 2001. For reference see *English Dictionary for Students* (1-901659-06-2)

# Unit Four

## 4f - Make a collocation

Start by reading through the sentences below. Then take one word from the box on the left and combine this with one from the box on the right to make a collocation. (Note that more than one pairing may be possible and also that some words appear more than once.) Then try to match your combinations with the spaces in the sentences below:

| |
|---|
| flatly • dense • military • atom |
| high • dedicated • mobile |
| embodies • Western • judicial |

| |
|---|
| proportion • fog • contradicted |
| the principle • system • bombs |
| his life • phones • culture • service |

1. An official spokesman _____ _____ allegations that the company had been responsible for the deaths of three employees, insisting that every precaution had been taken.

2. As more countries acquire the technology necessary to produce _____ _____ , the probability that they will be used again increases.

3. A _____ _____ of people released from prison continue to commit offences.

4. In some countries, _____ _____ has been rejected in favour of a more traditional view of society.

5. One major criticism of the _____ _____ in Britain is that there are not enough female judges.

6. Nelson Mandela has _____ _____ to achieving equality between black and white people in South Africa.

7. When there is heavy snow or _____ _____ , an airport may be closed down to prevent the possibility of an accident.

8. The policy of privatisation _____ _____ of a property-owning democracy.

9. Because of the growth in fax machines and _____ _____ , we will need more new telephone numbers.

10. In many European countries compulsory _____ _____ is the norm, whereas in Britain no one is required to join the armed forces.

> Don't forget to keep a record of the words and expressions that you have learnt, review your notes from time to time and try to use new vocabulary items whenever possible.

© Peter Collin Publishing 2001. For reference see *English Dictionary for Students* (1-901659-06-2)

## Vocabulary sheet

_____

_____

_____

_____

_____

_____

_____

_____

_____

_____

_____

_____

_____

_____

_____

_____

_____

_____

_____

_____

_____

_____

_____

_____

_____

_____

_____

_____

_____

_____

> **Don't forget to keep a record of the words and expressions that you have learnt, review your notes from time to time and try to use new vocabulary items whenever possible.**

© Peter Collin Publishing 2001. For reference see _English Dictionary for Students_ (1-901659-06-2)

# Unit Five

## 5a - Fill in the gaps

From the following list, use each word only once to complete the sentences below. Remember that in the case of nouns and verbs you may need to change the form of the word:

---

| | | | |
|---|---|---|---|
| aid (n) • | biology (n) • | edit (v) • | enlighten (v) |
| homogeneous (adj) • | overlap (v) • | stress (n) • | symptom (n) |
| trait (n) • | trivial (adj) • | version (n) • | x-rays (n) |

1. _____ are not simply used to photograph broken bones but also to fight against cancers within the body.

2. One big advantage of a word processor is that it allows you to check and then _____ your work easily.

3. The first witness accused the defendant of murder, but the second witness gave a very different _____ of events.

4. These experiments may seem _____ but they are in fact extremely important.

5. Of all the countries in the world, Japan may well be the most _____ as the great majority of its people are from the same race.

6. Heart disease can be caused by a bad diet (especially too much fat), inadequate exercise and too much _____ .

7. With the _____ of new medical techniques, couples who were previously unable to have children may now be able to start a family.

8. Headaches may just be the result of tiredness but can be a _____ of a more serious problem.

9. Jealousy is one of the most unpleasant human _____ .

10. She found physics easy because some of the course _____ with the maths she had studied at school.

11. _____ can be defined simply as the study of life.

12. Two students had great difficulty in solving the equation, but luckily their tutor was able to _____ them.

© Peter Collin Publishing 2001. For reference see *English Dictionary for Students* (1-901659-06-2)

## 5b - Choose the right word

**In each of the sentences below, decide which of the words in *bold* is more suitable.**

1. During the process known as photosynthesis, plants soak *up/absorb* $CO_2$ and release oxygen.

2. So many *contrary/unlike* opinions were expressed that no agreement was possible.

3. The United Nations representative managed to *secure/acquire* agreement between the two sides who had been fighting over an area of land rich in oil.

4. Although one of the prisoners refused to *respond/answer* to any questions, each of the others made a full confession.

5. Adjectives (big, green), verbs (come, go), conjunctions (and, but) and prepositions (to, in, for) are all *categories/groups* of words.

6. Divorce arouses such strong feelings that it is difficult to remain *honest/objective* and logical about the best way to tackle this problem.

7. The opening of a new car factory *stimulated/aroused* the local economy and improved employment possibilities.

8. When the government tried to *implement/start* new employment legislation, there was a general strike.

9. During times of war, governments usually *stop/suppress* any newspaper reports which contain bad news.

10. Examination candidates are not allowed to take eat, drink, smoke or talk for the *time/duration* of the examination.

11. The UK Government can decide to *suspend/expel* an overseas student who does not have a visa and refuse permission for the student to return.

12. Of all recent inventions, it is perhaps the motor car which has *transformed/modified* our lives more than anything else.

*Don't forget to keep a record of the words and expressions that you have learnt, review your notes from time to time and try to use new vocabulary items whenever possible.*

© Peter Collin Publishing 2001. For reference see *English Dictionary for Students* (1-901659-06-2)

# Unit Five

## 5c - Finish the sentence

**Choose the best ending for each of the sentence extracts below from the list underneath:**

1. The European Union has insisted that all new aircraft *incorporate*...

2. In today's economy, full-time permanent *jobs*...

3. Most British students used to receive a *grant*...

4. The police officer *denied*...

5. At the end of a quotation, remember to put in *parentheses*...

6. Because the universe is so *vast,*...

7. The measurements taken by researchers must be *accurate*...

8. Religion has many aspects, one of which is to provide a *code*...

9. Although many elderly people *retain*...

10. At university, it is best to use a formal, impersonal *style*...

11. Some clothes can be made from *synthetic*...

12. Inside the hydrogen atom, there is one *electron*...

---

a.   ...otherwise the conclusions they come to will be useless.

b.   ...of conduct to show people how they should behave.

c.   ...that he had accepted money from any criminal group.

d.   ...moving around the proton at the centre.

e.   ...from the government to pay for costs such as rent, food and books.

f.   ...additional safety features.

g.   ...are disappearing to be replaced by part-time temporary employment.

h.   ...the authors name, the date and the page number: (Brown 1996:76).

i.   ...clear memories of their childhood, they may completely forget recent events.

j.   ...in your writing, and to avoid contractions such as isn't and doesn't.

k.   ...materials such as nylon as well as natural materials such as cotton.

l.   ...it is unlikely that man will be able travel to other galaxies.

> *Don't forget to keep a record of the words and expressions that you have learnt, review your notes from time to time and try to use new vocabulary items whenever possible.*

© Peter Collin Publishing 2001. For reference see *English Dictionary for Students* (1-901659-06-2)

## 5d - Word substitution

From the list below, choose one word which could be used to replace the language shown in *bold* without changing the meaning of the sentence. Remember that you may need to change the form or in some cases the grammatical class of the word:

---

| | | | |
|---|---|---|---|
| advocate (v) • | insist (v) • | contract (v) • | dictate (v) |
| graph (n) • | compound (n) • | preliminary (adj) | |
| retard (v) • | subtle (adj) • | tiny (adj) • | transfer (v) |

1. Those who **support** military service claim that it promotes discipline, while opponents argue that such service disrupts young peoples education.  _____

2. Most metals **shrink** as they become cooler.  _____

3. Although not all the votes have been counted, **initial** results suggest that the President has won the election.  _____

4. In spite of a massive advertising campaign, only a **very small** proportion of consumers made a permanent change in their buying habits.  _____

5. If you look at this second **chart**, you can see that unemployment has been in decline for the past six years.  _____

6. Although the factory had to be closed, all the employees were **relocated** to another factory belonging to the same company.  _____

7. Some organisations have a dress code which **lays down** what their employees should wear.  _____

8. Although the two cases seemed to be identical, one lawyer showed that there were some **slight** differences between them.  _____

9. One of the many effects of the hole in the ozone layer is that increased radiation will **delay** the growth of plants and lead to food shortages.  _____

10. Water is a **combination** of hydrogen and oxygen.  _____

11. The prisoner **said repeatedly** that he was innocent until he was released.  _____

---

*Don't forget to keep a record of the words and expressions that you have learnt, review your notes from time to time and try to use new vocabulary items whenever possible.*

**33**

© Peter Collin Publishing 2001. For reference see *English Dictionary for Students* (1-901659-06-2)

# Unit Five

## 5e - Choose the best word

**For each of the sentences here, choose the best word from *a, b* or *c*.**

1. As trade union membership has declined, the number of _____ and strikes has also decreased.

   *a. arguments*          *b. disagreements*          *c. disputes*

2. The role of the middle manager is not to formulate new policies but to _____ them.

   *a. manage*          *b. use*          *c. execute*

3. Engineers worked throughout the night to _____ electricity to homes whose supplies had been cut off by heavy snow.

   *a. reinstate*          *b. renew*          *c. restore*

4. Many athletes take extra vitamins as a(n) _____ to their diet when they are preparing for competition.

   *a. reinforcement*          *b. supplement*          *c. extension*

5. Police officers face many dangers, especially when they are _____ by violent criminals carrying weapons.

   *a. confronted*          *b. met*          *c. encountered*

6. The invention of printing allowed ideas to _____ much more quickly than before.

   *a. scatter*          *b. diffuse*          *c. disseminate*

7. In many cultures, it was traditionally believed that men were _____ to women, but this attitude has been changing rapidly in recent years.

   *a. better*          *b. inferior*          *c. superior*

8. In the early years, facilities for tourists were rather _____ , but now they are highly developed.

   *a. crude*          *b. rudimentary*          *c. uncomplicated*

9. Increasingly, post-graduate students are asked to become teaching assistants in order to _____ undergraduates.

   *a. instruct*          *b. drill*          *c. inform*

10. Cigarette packets on sale are required to carry a _____ clearly stating the dangers of smoking.

    *a. label*          *b. message*          *c. tag*

11. A defence lawyer has a duty to try to establish the innocence of his/her _____ .

    *a. patient*          *b. customer*          *c. client*

12. You can buy goods on the Internet with a credit card, but there is a danger of _____ if someone else obtains the number.

    *a. corruption*          *b. fraud*          *c. embezzlement*

© Peter Collin Publishing 2001. For reference see *English Dictionary for Students* (1-901659-06-2)

## 5f - Make a collocation

Start by reading through the sentences below. Then take one word from the box on the left and combine this with one from the box on the right to make a collocation. (Note that more than one pairing may be possible and also that some words appear more than once.) Then try to match your combinations with the spaces in the sentences below:

| |
|---|
| force of • err on • lines • abstract |
| imposed • crisis of • research • at regular |
| within a • legitimate • perpetrated |

| |
|---|
| a ban • concern • thought • confidence |
| crimes • gravity • intervals • the side |
| of caution • intersect • institutes • radius |

1. Most academic journals are published _____ _____ , perhaps every month or every quarter.

2. While it is probably true they are not capable of _____ _____ , most animals appear to experience a range of emotions.

3. There is a tradition that a falling apple helped Newton develop his theory about the _____ _____ .

4. In the 1970's, the price of oil increased dramatically, causing an international economic _____ _____ .

5. Most people accept that fighting against terrorism is a _____ _____ of any government.

6. Because of the danger of an explosion, everyone who was _____ _____ of 500 metres of the bomb was evacuated.

7. Before publishing the results of new research, it is better to _____ _____ and recheck the results.

8. On this graph, where the two _____ _____ we find the ideal balance.

9. Following the rise in violence, the government _____ _____ on the private ownership of guns.

10. Because of the work of _____ _____ , there is increasing hope that effective treatments for AIDS will soon be available.

11. He _____ _____ which were so terrible that a massive manhunt was launched by the police to find him.

© Peter Collin Publishing 2001. For reference see *English Dictionary for Students* (1-901659-06-2)

# Unit Five

## Vocabulary sheet

*Don't forget to keep a record of the words and expressions that you have learnt, review your notes from time to time and try to use new vocabulary items whenever possible.*

© Peter Collin Publishing 2001. For reference see *English Dictionary for Students* (1-901659-06-2)

## 6a - Fill in the gaps

**From the following list, use each word only once to complete the sentences below. Remember that in the case of nouns and verbs you may need to change the form of the word:**

---

| | | | |
|---|---|---|---|
| academic (adj) • | arouse (v) • | benefit (n) • | compute (v) |
| contend (v) • | degenerate (v) • | hierarchy (n) • | instinct (n) |
| interlocking (adj) • | metabolism (n) • | radical (adj) • | strata (n) |

1. Students at university are encouraged to play sports or join clubs in addition to following their _____ studies.

2. Animals with a very fast _____ have to eat very frequently and do not live very long.

3. _____ of rock likely to contain oil have recently been located under the ice-sheet in Antarctica.

4. The fact that the car was being driven very badly _____ the policeman's suspicions, and so he made the driver stop.

5. All the equipment is made up of _____ pieces which can be easily assembled in weightless conditions.

6. An organisational chart shows the company _____ , from the managers at the top down to the employees at the bottom.

7. During the 1930's, President Roosevelt introduced _____ , new policies to solve the American unemployment problem.

8. We can make machines which can _____ huge numbers of mathematical problems, but it is still too early to claim that machines can actually think for themselves.

9. Some people emphasize the _____ of new technology, while others stress the disadvantages.

10. The argument became so heated that it soon _____ into accusations of dishonesty and corruption.

11. By _____ , a young baby will start to cry if it is hungry, cold, or in pain.

12. Some religious groups _____ that Darwin's theory of evolution is completely wrong.

© Peter Collin Publishing 2001. For reference see *English Dictionary for Students* (1-901659-06-2)

# Unit Six

## 6b - Choose the right word

In each of the sentences below, decide which of the words in *bold* is more suitable:

1. In India, Mahatma Gandhi refused all food and indeed nearly died in his *protest/complaint* against British control of his country.
2. If you are taking medicine, you should avoid alcohol as the two may *interact/cooperate* and make you ill.
3. *Medium-/Middle-sized* companies are often more flexible than larger organisations.
4. Government safety inspectors found *abnormal/unlikely* levels of radiation in the area around the nuclear power station.
5. More than 30,000 people *participated/contributed* in the experiment.
6. Most universities *oblige/force* overseas students to take an English language test before they start their course.
7. Companies which cannot adapt to changing situations very often go into *decline/decrease.*
8. The *tone/style* of the meeting was rather serious and formal.
9. Many police officers argue that ex-prisoners *commit/perform* as much crime after they come out of prison as before they went in.
10. Studying a new subject means having to learn a lot of new *vocabulary/terminology,* and these special words can make progress very slow.
11. He is such a powerful boxer that all his opponents are in *awe/fright* of him.
12. The *appeal/claim* by protesters for more money to be invested in education was rejected by the Government.

## 6c - Finish the sentence

Choose the best ending for each of the sentence extracts below from the list underneath:

1. The decision to expand the airport has caused a great deal of *controversy,*...
2. The murder was a very strange case but the most striking *aspect*...
3. All new cars on the market today have to *conform*...
4. The Pope in Rome is — according to the *doctrine*...
5. Cars are not allowed to enter many *civic* ...
6. The police *accompanied* ...
7. The film was made on a very low budget, so all the *minor*...
8. Mercury is the smallest *planet*...
9. Whatever type of job you may be *contemplating,*...
10. At the end of the process, any parts which are not of *uniform*...
11. When selecting new employees, it is important to ignore *subjective*...
12. Buildings in places such as California have to be *reinforced*...
13. In the United Kingdom, Queen Victoria *reigned*...

a. ...the witness to the court to ensure that he would be safe.
b. ...was the fact that the murderers were both under 10 years old.
c. ...centres today, because of pollution and congestion problems.
d. ...to the same safety and pollution regulations.
e. ...but construction has already started and should be completed soon.
f. ...of the Catholic Church — the representative of God here on Earth.
g. ...the university careers service can give you advice.
h. ...roles were played by people from the local area.
i. ...in our solar system.
j. ...for most of the previous century, before her son became king in 1901.
k. ...shape and size are rejected and sent back for recycling.
l. ...impressions and to base decisions on facts instead.
m. ...so that they will not collapse in the event of an earthquake.

© Peter Collin Publishing 2001. For reference see *English Dictionary for Students* (1-901659-06-2)

## 6d - Word substitution

From the list below, choose one word which could be used in place of the language shown in *bold* without changing the meaning of the sentence. Remember that you may need to change the form or in some cases the grammatical class of the word:

---

| | | | | |
|---|---|---|---|---|
| assist (v) • | clarify (v) • | converse (v) • | demonstrate (v) • | extract (v) |
| incline (v) • | propagate (v) • | propensity (n) • | sustain (v) • | urban (adj) |

1. The lecturer tried to **explain more clearly** her point by using another example more familiar to her students.

2. It is impossible to **grow** crops without an adequate supply of water.

3. By the age of three, most children are able to **talk** with an adult in a limited fashion.

4. Because of unhappy childhood experiences, he is **disposed** to believe that most people are basically very selfish.

5. During examinations, students are not allowed to talk to or **help** other students in any way.

6. Students should not read every page of a book but instead identify and then **take out** only those ideas which are relevant.

7. Some students will stay up all night to finish their work, but it is impossible to **maintain** this for very long and so it is not recommended.

8. One of the main causes of the increase in **inner-city** lawlessness is the number of young people dependent on drugs.

9. Heavy smokers have a **tendency** to develop lung cancer and other serious illnesses.

10. In recent environmental protests, agitators have **protested** against the building of new roads.

---

*Don't forget to keep a record of the words and expressions that you have learnt, review your notes from time to time and try to use new vocabulary items whenever possible.*

© Peter Collin Publishing 2001. For reference see *English Dictionary for Students* (1-901659-06-2)

# Unit Six

## 6e - Choose the best word

For each of the sentences here, choose the best word from *a, b* or *c*.

1. Wearing a seatbelt when travelling in a car is now a _____ requirement in many countries, and people who do not so may be punished in the courts.
   *a. legal*                 *b. compulsory*          *c. binding*

2. Because the strikers still refused to return to work, the employers agreed reluctantly to _____ their pay offer to the workers.
   *a. rewrite*               *b. revise*              *c. reproduce*

3. The age at which a child becomes _____ in the United Kingdom is 18.
   *a. a person*              *b. an adult*            *c. an individual*

4. Many scientists believe that most dinosaurs were killed as a result of a huge meteor which _____ with the Earth 65 million years ago.
   *a. crashed*               *b. hit*                 *c. collided*

5. The journalist asked the Prime Minister repeatedly about the scandal but he refused to _____ on it.
   *a. comment*               *b. mention*             *c. discuss*

6. Despite a great deal of evidence to the contrary, tobacco companies _____ the public for years that smoking was not a direct cause of cancer.
   *a. promised*              *b. assured*             *c. persuaded*

7. While South Korea has _____ over the last fifty years, North Korea is still relatively underdeveloped.
   *a. succeeded*             *b. prospered*           *c. achieved*

8. In most companies, employees receive extra _____ if they do extra work.
   *a. income*               *b. revenue*             *c. salary*

9. Following unification, the German government decided to move the capital from Bonn and _____ it once more in Berlin.
   *a. position*             *b. locate*              *c. place*

10. There are many parts of the world which are _____ enough to produce food but do not have enough water.
    *a. productive*           *b. fertile*             *c. agricultural*

11. Most universities have trained counsellors who can reassure and _____ students who have academic or personal problems.
    *a. console*              *b. sympathise*          *c. cheer*

12. The _____ of world trade has increased enormously during the twentieth century.
    *a. size*                 *b. volume*              *c. scope*

13. To improve teamworking, students are often asked to _____ to produce a group report or presentation together.
    *a. assist*               *b. unite*               *c. cooperate*

© Peter Collin Publishing 2001. For reference see *English Dictionary for Students* (1-901659-06-2)

## 6f - Make a collocation

**Start by reading through the sentences below. Then take one word from the box on the left and combine this with one from the box on the right to make a collocation. (Note that more than one pairing may be possible and also that some words appear more than once.) Then try to match your combinations with the spaces in the sentences below:**

| | |
|---|---|
| keep • identical • attain • virtual<br><br>niche • brief • under • endless<br><br>southern • economic • go off at | interlude • their goals • reality • market<br><br>a tangent • twins • your nerve • cycle<br><br>sanctions • the microscope • hemisphere |

1. When you look at your exam paper, try to _____ _____ and don't panic; concentrate on what you can do!

2. Following the Gulf War, _____ _____ were imposed on Iraq to prevent the sale of oil.

3. Sometimes, university life just seems to be an _____ _____ of assignment after assignment.

4. In spite of equal opportunities policies, women are still not able to _____ _____ as easily as men in terms of reaching the top positions.

5. Some lecturers are difficult to follow because they _____ _____ and talk about something completely different.

6. Most _____ _____ not only look alike but also behave and even dress similarly.

7. _____ _____ is now so advanced that pilots train with it.

8. Some insects are so small that they can only really be seen properly _____ _____ .

9. The countries in the _____ _____ are in general poorer than those in the northern.

10. After two months of non-stop fighting there was a _____ _____ of peace on Christmas Day before the fighting started again.

11. While the Volkswagen car was designed to appeal to the masses, the Rolls Royce has only ever been aimed at a _____ _____ .

© Peter Collin Publishing 2001. For reference see *English Dictionary for Students* (1-901659-06-2)

# Unit Six

## Vocabulary sheet

_____

_____

_____

_____

_____

_____

_____

_____

_____

_____

_____

_____

_____

_____

_____

_____

_____

_____

_____

_____

_____

_____

_____

*Don't forget to keep a record of the words and expressions that you have learnt, review
your notes from time to time and try to use new vocabulary items whenever possible.*

© Peter Collin Publishing 2001. For reference see *English Dictionary for Students* (1-901659-06-2)

## 7a - Fill in the gaps

From the following list, use each word only once to complete the sentences below. Remember that in the case of nouns and verbs you may need to change the form of the word:

| | | | |
|---|---|---|---|
| adolescent (n) • | affiliate (v) • | aristocracy (n) • | repudiate (v) |
| collapse (v) • | commodity (n) • | democracy (n) • | dissolve (v) |
| friction (n) • | invoke (v) • | muscle (n) • | cell (n) • saint (n) |

1. _____ are the tiny, basic building blocks from which all living creatures are made up.

2. In many countries, there has been a worrying increase in the number of _____ taking drugs.

3. Without any warning, the building _____ killing more than 300 people inside.

4. In times of unemployment, _____ can arise between people who have jobs and those who do not.

5. _____ markets allow traders to buy and sell raw materials such as cotton, steel and sugar.

6. In order to become more powerful, trade unions usually _____ to a national union organisation.

7. Individuals who have become very rich through business usually also have a lot of political _____ and can therefore influence political decisions.

8. Sugar and salt _____ easily in water.

9. At the public enquiry, the Managing Director _____ all suggestions that the company had tried to avoid responsibility for the accident.

10. He was more than a national hero; in fact, most people looked up to him almost as a _____ .

11. As a result of the revolution of 1917, the royal family and the _____ in Russia were overthrown and a communist government was installed.

12. Many political scientists argue that it is impossible to have a truly modern economy without _____ and a more open society.

13. In the USA, citizens can _____ the right to silence if they do not want to answer a question in court.

## 7b - Choose the right word

**In each of the sentences below, decide which word in *bold* is more suitable**

1. Although unemployment was falling, the economy remained *depressed/distressed* because consumers still felt insecure about their jobs.

2. Computer equipment can become *obsolete/antique* very quickly because new technology emerges so fast.

3. In swimming pools, there is a slight *odour/fragrance* because of the chlorine in the water.

© Peter Collin Publishing 2001. For reference see *English Dictionary for Students* (1-901659-06-2)

# Unit Seven

4. Some religious groups are strongly opposed to modern science, and *refute/contradict* even well-established theories such as evolution.

5. When designers choose material for making new clothes, they are particularly interested in the colour and the *touch/texture* of the material.

6. Increasingly, it seems that politicians who are *dogmatic/pragmatic* rather than rigid in their views tend to be more successful.

7. There are so many aircraft using Heathrow Airport these days that the noise is almost *incessant/eternal.*

8. Recent tests show that girls are getting higher *scores/results* than boys in most school subjects.

9. The *creditors/debtors* of a company are those individuals or organisations to whom that company owes money.

10. The defendant is allowed to *discuss/confer* with his/her lawyer before and during the trial.

11. Before the election, all the main political parties tried to explain their main *policy/line* to the voters through television broadcasts and newspaper advertisements.

12. Some species of birds *migrate/commute* from North Africa to Britain.

13. If the *pattern/configuration* of the control panel in an aircraft makes it difficult for the pilot to read the instruments, the chance of an accident will increase.

## 7c - Finish the sentence

**Choose the best ending for each of the sentence extracts below from the list underneath:**

1. One branch of mathematics is *geometry*...

2. Electrical equipment is usually supplied with a *fuse,*...

3. Muslims have a system of *divine*...

4. In 1991, President Saddam Hussein of Iraq *invaded*...

5. The new management team managed to *revive*...

6. When we talk about *sociology,*...

7. People in Japan enjoy a great deal of *affluence*...

8. In this lecture, I just want to give you a brief *sketch*...

9. Fifty years after the Second World War, a state of tension *prevailed*...

10. Like the United States Congress, the UK *Parliament*...

11. Early computers were very *cumbersome*...

12. The Government has reduced the number of ships in the *navy*...

---

a. ...due to the economic growth of the last 30 years.

b. ...which is concerned for example with lines and the shapes and angles they make.

c. ...we are interested in the study of society and how people behave within it.

d. ...but today they are much smaller.

e. ...law based on the Koran.

f. ...the neighbouring country of Kuwait.

g. ...which will blow if a fault develops.

h. ...and concentrated resources on the airforce instead.

i. ...between the communist and capitalist worlds, called the Cold War.

j. ...rather than speak in great detail about this new topic.

k. ...is responsible for making laws.

l. ...the company, which many had thought was beyond hope.

© Peter Collin Publishing 2001. For reference see *English Dictionary for Students* (1-901659-06-2)

## 7d - Word substitution

From the list below, choose one word which could be used in place of the language shown in *bold* without changing the meaning of the sentence. Remember that you may need to change the form or in some cases the grammatical class of the word:

---

alcohol (n) • competence (n) • conserve (v) • corporate (adj)

defer (v) • domestic (adj) • fraction (n) • horror (n) • incentive (n)

negotiate (v) • peasant (n) • prudence (n) • rhythm (n)

---

1. In many types of music, some kind of drum is used to provide the *beat.*

2. Some products are exported and may not be available at all in the *home* market.

3. There is growing pressure on governments to *protect* forests and wild animals.

4. If you wish to travel or work before studying, it is possible to *postpone* your entry to university by one year.

5. Companies often give employees *inducements* such as bonuses and pay rises to encourage them to work harder.

6. It is now common *organisational* policy for a company to have a mission statement explaining the aim of the organisation.

7. Only a *small proportion* of the competitors in the Olympic Games actually win a medal.

8. Agoraphobia can be defined as a *dread* of large, open spaces, its opposite being claustrophobia.

9. During the 1930's, the sale of *strong drink* was illegal in the USA, and yet consumption of drink actually increased.

10. I am impressed by her business sense, and I thought that her decision not to expand the company showed a great deal of *wisdom.*

11. Rather than use force, the authorities tried to *have discussions* with the terrorists to secure the release of the hostages.

12. Increasingly, employers are keen to recruit people who have at least a basic *ability* in computing.

13. The 1949 revolution in China was successful because the *agricultural workers* and farmers gave their support to the communists.

© Peter Collin Publishing 2001. For reference see *English Dictionary for Students* (1-901659-06-2)

# Unit Seven

## 7e - Choose the best word

For each of the sentences here, choose the best word from: *a, b, or c.*

1. In any large company, the _____ Department is responsible for managing money within that organisation.
   a. *Finance*          b. *Monetary*          c. *Economic*

2. Some political parties want to _____ the process by which we vote in general elections so as to make it more representative.
   a. *rewrite*          b. *redraw*          c. *reform*

3. In the next century, the _____ of Asia will become the most significant sector of the world economic market.
   a. *region*          b. *continent*          c. *area*

4. Mad cow disease was probably caused by allowing cows to eat nerve _____ , from sheep and other cows.
   a. *tissue*          b. *flesh*          c. *matter*

5. In the US today, more and more children live with one parent, and yet the _____ of the two-parent family still exists.
   a. *icon*          b. *stereotype*          c. *symbol*

6. The study of _____ has been helped considerably by the Hubble telescope, the only telescope up in space.
   a. *astronomy*          b. *astrology*          c. *astronomer*

7. In the Second World War, Switzerland declared that it would remain _____ and not take part in any of the fighting.
   a. *neutral*          b. *disinterested*          c. *impartial*

8. The roots of a plant absorb water and _____ from the soil in which it grows.
   a. *food*          b. *nutrition*          c. *nutrients*

9. Because of modern communications, it is increasingly common for people to _____ business without actually meeting.
   a *perform*          b. *transact*          c. *make*

10. According to the _____ , the building should be ready for use by the end of the year.
    a. *timing*          b. *schedule*          c. *time*

11. Many food products carry a 'sell by' date since they _____ over time and become unusable.
    a. *degrade*          b. *degenerate*          c. *corrupt*

12. A simple everyday example of the _____ is the standard postcard.
    a. *triangle*          b. *square*          c. *rectangle*

© Peter Collin Publishing 2001. For reference see *English Dictionary for Students* (1-901659-06-2)

## 7f - Make a collocation

**Start by reading through the sentences below. Then take one word from the box on the left and combine this with one from the box on the right to make a collocation. (Note that more than one pairing may be possible and also that some words appear more than once.) Then try to match your combinations with the spaces in the sentences below:**

| | | |
|---|---|---|
| sibling • thermal • a code | | |
| contingent • pleaded • salt | | |
| precipitated • intermediate • US | | |
| political • campaign • colloquial | | |

| | | |
|---|---|---|
| not guilty • a crisis • energy | | |
| crystals • stages • Congress | | |
| rivalry • of terror • of ethics | | |
| spectrum • upon • language | | |

1. The shortage of oil in the 1970's _____ _____ in the world economy.

2. In areas with active volcanoes, the _____ _____ from underground hot water supplies can be used to produce electricity.

3. The water evaporated, leaving behind only _____ _____ .

4. Although he _____ _____ , the court sentenced him to three years in prison.

5. Doctors have a _____ _____ which requires them to act in the best interest of their patients.

6. _____ _____ refers to the competition which often exists between the children in a family for the attention and love of their parents.

7. Although there has been some success, the discussions are still only in the _____ _____ .

8. The results of the vote showed agreement across the _____ _____ , both on the extreme left and extreme right.

9. One extreme political group started a _____ _____ , including hijacking, kidnapping and bombing.

10. When speaking, we tend to use _____ _____ , but in academic writing we need to be much more formal.

11. The decision by Japanese companies to invest in the UK was _____ _____ Britain being part of the European Union.

12. The _____ _____ is made up of the House of Representatives and the Senate.

---

*Don't forget to keep a record of the words and expressions that you have learnt, review your notes from time to time and try to use new vocabulary items whenever possible.*

© Peter Collin Publishing 2001. For reference see *English Dictionary for Students* (1-901659-06-2)

# Unit Seven

## Vocabulary sheet

*Don't forget to keep a record of the words and expressions that you have learnt, review your notes from time to time and try to use new vocabulary items whenever possible.*

© Peter Collin Publishing 2001. For reference see *English Dictionary for Students* (1-901659-06-2)

## 8a - Fill in the gaps

From the following list, use each word only once to complete the sentences below. Remember that in the case of nouns and verbs you may need to change the form of the word:

---

aggregate (adj)  •  fraternal (adj)  •  lens (n)  •  liable (adj)

nuclear (adj)  •  oxygen (n)  •  pendulum (n)  •  postulate (v)

reproduce  (v)  •  subordinate  (adj)  •  supreme  (adj)

---

1.  By putting two _____ together, it is possible to make a simple telescope.

2.  If students do not attend lectures, they are _____ to fail their examinations.

3.  The _____ value of all the companies in the group was in excess of $250 million.

4.  Periods of high economic growth tend to be followed by low growth, followed by more high growth again, like a _____ .

5.  The _____ Court in the United States is the highest and most important court in the country.

6.  _____ energy provides 70% of the electricity used in France, more than in any other country.

7.  In any strike action by a trade union, _____ support from workers in other unions can be very important for it to succeed.

8.  In this company, the supervisors are _____ to the inspectors, who in turn report to the Production Manager.

9.  About 20% of the atmosphere is made up of _____ , which is vital for life on Earth.

10. By law in the UK, you are allowed to _____ up to 10% of a book for your own personal study.

11. Karl Marx _____ that the structure of a society is determined by the economic structure of that society.

## 8b - Choose the right word

In each of the sentences below, decide which word in *bold* is more suitable:

---

1.  In many cases, countries which may have been enemies in the past are often *allies/friends* today.

2.  If a student does not *follow/adhere* to the regulations concerning examinations, he/she may fail.

3.  In his book *The Plague,* Camus uses the disease mentioned in the title as a *metaphor/simile* to represent fascism and other extreme political ideas.

4.  Some students complained because the extra lecture *coincided/synchronized* with one of their religious festivals.

5.  The former President's personality was so strong that her influence *invaded/pervaded* every aspect of political life.

© Peter Collin Publishing 2001. For reference see *English Dictionary for Students* (1-901659-06-2)

# Unit Eight

6. Some students are *reluctant/unhappy* to ask questions because they are shy.

7. The *contents/index* at the back of a book allows the reader to find specific information.

8. In some parts of the world, children have to work very long hours, to the *detriment/expense* of their education and even their health.

9. The idea that HIV and AIDS only affect homosexuals is a complete *error/fallacy.*

10. The number of people living on our planet is on an upward *trend/pattern* and is expected to top 10 billion in the years to come.

11. While our reserves of oil and coal are *fixed/finite*, energy sources such as the wind or the sun will in effect never end.

# 8c - Finish the sentence

**Choose the best ending for each of the sentence extracts below from the list underneath:**

1. It is very important that a child's *linguistic*...

2. Teachers have noticed an increase in *aggression,*...

3. The US Navy has the largest *fleet*...

4. Medical researchers managed to *correlate*...

5. University courses used to be very *rigid*...

6. From a very early age, children develop a *spatial*...

7. During the Korean War, communist countries *aligned*...

8. Some countries have a president, while others have a *monarch,*...

9. The European Union has reduced most of the *bureaucracy*...

10. Because of radio telescopes, we can now *detect*...

11. It is vital to make sure that the structure of a bridge will not *oscillate*...

a. ...awareness allowing them to understand where things are around them.

b. ...which may be caused by the food which children are eating.

c. ...themselves with the North, with capitalist countries aiding the South.

d. ...either a king or queen.

e. ...of ships in the world.

f. ...abilities develop fully so that it can communicate and learn.

g. ...up and down or from side to side, as this would cause it to collapse.

h. ...distant stars which are invisible from Earth.

i. ...and offered students no real choice or flexibility.

j. ...associated with customs, thereby simplifying trade regulations.

k. ...asbestos to lung cancer and other respiratory diseases many years ago.

© Peter Collin Publishing 2001. For reference see *English Dictionary for Students* (1-901659-06-2)

## 8d - Word substitution

From the list below, choose one word which could be used in place of the language shown in *bold* without changing the meaning of the sentence. Remember that you may need to change the form or in some cases the grammatical class of the word:

| | | | |
|---|---|---|---|
| allude (v) • | cater (v) • | discern (v) • | drug (n) |
| evolve (v) • | launch (v) • | proclaim (v) • | rebel (n) |
| territory (n) • | testify (v) • | utilise (v) | |

1. In the twentieth century, Britain **developed gradually** from an industrial economy into a service economy.

2. The independence of the United States of America was **announced** in 1776.

3. Many companies in the developed world are trying to **provide** for older customers as the proportion of young people decreases.

4. The witness was so nervous that he refused to **give evidence** when the case came to court.

5. There is a very real danger that **medicines** currently used to treat infection will become completely ineffective if they are used too often and indiscriminately.

6. One of the most important skills to learn as a student is how to **make use of** your time effectively.

7. Despite the efforts of the doctors, it was not possible to **notice** any real improvement in the condition of the patient.

8. Most animals will attack other animals which try to enter their **space.**

9. In the course of a trial, lawyers are forbidden to mention or even **refer** to any previous criminal activity the accused may have been responsible for in the past.

10. The government has decided to **initiate** an investigation into the increase in deaths from drugs.

11. **Revolutionaries** overpowered the troops holding the radio station so that they could announce the change of government to the people.

---

*Don't forget to keep a record of the words and expressions that you have learnt, review your notes from time to time and try to use new vocabulary items whenever possible.*

---

© Peter Collin Publishing 2001. For reference see *English Dictionary for Students* (1-901659-06-2)

# Unit Eight

## 8e - Choose the best word

**For each of the sentences here, choose the best word from *a, b or c*:**

1. Some plants _____ a sweet, sticky liquid to attract insects.
   *a. exude*          *b. leak*          *c. drip*

2. To cut down on costs, the university _____ each student a limit of 500 pages of computer printing.
   *a. allots*          *b. gives*          *c. allocates*

3. If children are _____ of love and security they may have problems in later life.
   *a. stripped*          *b. deprived*          *c. denied*

4. The decision of the university to close the swimming pool at weekends _____ an angry reaction among students.
   *a. created*          *b. provoked*          *c. stimulated*

5. Students on the new technology course became very _____ at the lack of suitable books in the library.
   *a. despondent*          *b. frustrated*          *c. sad*

6. In the seventeenth century, William Harvey showed that blood _____ around the body on a continuous basis.
   *a. flows*          *b. circulates*          *c. pours*

7. The G7 is a _____ of the world's seven richest countries.
   *a. division*          *b. club*          *c. league*

8. According to witnesses, some UFO's can appear and disappear again as if by _____ .
   *a  trickery*          *b  magic*          *c. miracle*

9. Many political parties support the introduction of a common _____ , accepted all over Europe.
   *a. money*          *b. finance*          *c. currency*

10. The decision of the House of Commons surprised no one, as the politicians simply voted along _____ lines: the left-wing all supported the Prime Minister, and the right-wing all opposed him.
    *a. partisan*          *b. factional*          *c. biased*

---

*Don't forget to keep a record of the words and expressions that you have learnt, review your notes from time to time and try to use new vocabulary items whenever possible.*

© Peter Collin Publishing 2001. For reference see *English Dictionary for Students* (1-901659-06-2)

## 8f - Make a collocation

**Start by reading through the sentences below. Then take one word from the box on the left and combine this with one from the box on the right to make a collocation. (Note that more than one pairing may be possible and also that some words appear more than once.) Then try to match your combinations with the spaces in the sentences below:**

| | |
|---|---|
| solar • imperial • dissipate | against • energy • money |
| on the premise • Peace • sex and | waste of time • violence • control • their |
| legislate • invest • give • utter | consent • power • that • Treaty |

1. There is very little evidence to suggest that _____ _____ as portrayed on television and in film actually cause antisocial behaviour.

2. Many students make the mistake of reading without considering first why they are reading, which just _____ _____ for no good reason.

3. The _____ _____ signed at Versailles marked the end of the First World War.

4. One obvious source of energy is _____ _____ , since the sun produces so much heat.

5. It is almost impossible to _____ _____ people who use the Internet for criminal purposes.

6. Most of the students complained that the lectures were an _____ _____ because it was impossible to understand the lecturer.

7. During the nineteenth century, perhaps a quarter of the world's population was under British _____ _____ .

8. Some years ago, seat-belt legislation was introduced, _____ _____ this would reduce the number of serious injuries.

9. One common complaint is that companies do not _____ _____ in new developments for the long-term future.

10. In some countries, if both pairs of parents _____ _____ , young people can get married below the age of 18.

---

*Don't forget to keep a record of the words and expressions that you have learnt, review your notes from time to time and try to use new vocabulary items whenever possible.*

---

© Peter Collin Publishing 2001. For reference see *English Dictionary for Students* (1-901659-06-2)

# Unit Eight

## Vocabulary sheet

_Don't forget to keep a record of the words and expressions that you have learnt, review your notes from time to time and try to use new vocabulary items whenever possible._

© Peter Collin Publishing 2001. For reference see _English Dictionary for Students_ (1-901659-06-2)

## 9a - Fill in the gaps

From the following list, use each word only once to complete the sentences below. Remember that in the case of nouns and verbs you may need to change the form of the word:

---

| | | | |
|---|---|---|---|
| acid (n) • | battery (n) • | breed (v) • | carbon (n) |
| prince (n) • | integer (n) • | lustre (n) • | matrix (n) |
| molecule (n) • | illuminate (n) • | stationary (adj) | |

---

1. The element _____ is all around us, in the air we breathe, even in the pencils with which we write.

2. In the United Kingdom, _____.Charles will one day replace Queen Elizabeth II as the monarch.

3. In this exercise, just use _____ , and don't bother with any fractions or decimal points.

4. The music was really quite boring and had no real _____ .

5. Two atoms of oxygen and an atom of hydrogen together produce one _____ of water.

6. A great deal of research has shown that poverty, lack of education and unemployment can _____ social unrest.

7. Astronomers' work is becoming more difficult as the night sky is increasingly _____ by electric street lighting from urban areas.

8. Until 400 years ago, it was believed that the Earth was _____ , and that the Sun moved around the Earth.

9. One of the biggest problems for electric cars is that the _____ they use for power are rather heavy.

10. Car batteries also have to be handled with care as they often contain an _____ which can burn holes in clothes or even cause injury.

11. The grid on the left of your handout is known as a square _____ , as the number of columns and the number of rows are the same.

---

*Don't forget to keep a record of the words and expressions that you have learnt, review your notes from time to time and try to use new vocabulary items whenever possible.*

© Peter Collin Publishing 2001. For reference see *English Dictionary for Students* (1-901659-06-2)

# Unit Nine

## 9b - Choose the right word

In each of the sentences below, decide which of the words in *bold* is more suitable:

1. Most universities have a special *fund/finance* for students who have run out of money and need help.
2. The prediction that we will completely *tire/exhaust* our reserves of oil in the not too distant future seems now to be incorrect.
3. Because he lied to his colleagues and family about his *girlfriend/mistress,* the minister destroyed not only his career but also his marriage.
4. Because of the rise in the number of prisoners, the whole *penal/punishment* system will have to be changed.
5. After six weeks trapped in the embassy, the hostages were finally *emancipated/liberated.*
6. Sometimes a piece of music can *evoke/provoke* very strong memories and emotions.
7. The biggest issue on which the two parties' policies *divide/diverge* is the amount of money to be spent on education.
8. In some countries, the police regularly use *torture/torment* to force prisoners to give them information.
9. The most successful students are probably those who have a strong *integral/intrinsic* interest in their subject, as opposed to those who simply want a degree.
10. In the 1970's, Saudi Arabia and other oil-rich states *accumulated/collected* vast sums of money through the sale of oil.

## 9c - Finish the sentence

Choose the best ending for each of the sentence extracts below from the list underneath:

1. She won the championship by a *margin...*
2. Examples of animals imported by man replacing the *indigenous...*
3. In 1685, an aristocrat by the name of the *Duke...*
4. Civil war may break out very quickly if different *factions...*
5. Plants can be *subdivided...*
6. When you write an essay, you must *confine...*
7. Because of the special *apparatus ...*
8. From the Vatican in Rome, the *Pope...*
9. The organisation of the department is really quite *amorphous,...*
10. The Romans built a large number of castles or *forts...*
11. Because of their high price, some students are not *averse...*

a. ...and so the people in it are free to work on what they like, when they like.
b. ...required, higher fees are charged for science and technology courses.
c. ...to stealing books from the library.
d. ...yourself to giving relevant ideas and information only.
e. ...of Monmouth led a rebellion against the English king.
f. ...in a country start fighting each other.
g. ...called 'castra,' which we now see in place names like Lancaster.
h. ...species already living there can be seen in all countries.
i. ...of only one point.
j. ...has the power to influence the lives of millions of Catholics.
k. ...into several different families.

© Peter Collin Publishing 2001. For reference see *English Dictionary for Students* (1-901659-06-2)

## 9d - Word substitution

From the list below, choose one word which could be used in place of the language shown in **bold** without changing the meaning of the sentence. Remember that you may need to change the form or in some cases the grammatical class of the word:

| | | | |
|---|---|---|---|
| ambiguity (n) • | annual (adj) • | construe (v) • | displace (v) |
| efficient (adj) • | innate (adj) • | material (n) • | orbit (v) |
| residue (n) • | reverberate (v) • | suspend (v) | |

1. The **yearly** external examiners' meeting is held at the end of every academic year to discuss the examination papers which the students have written.

2. He is a very pleasant colleague, and very **proficient** at his job.

3. The workers went on strike as they **viewed** the management's plans as an attack on their job security.

4. Some psychologists think our language ability is **intrinsic,** while others think that we know nothing about language at birth.

5. Because of reports that the meat was not safe, all sales were **halted** until more tests could be carried out.

6. Aluminium is a very suitable **substance** for aircraft because it is light and strong.

7. The Space Shuttle **circles** the Earth once every 10 hours.

8. The noise of the explosion **echoed** through the empty streets.

9. Most of the money was spent on salaries, with the **remainder** used for new equipment.

10. Some industry experts believe that the Internet will **supplant** television and all programmes will be viewed from a computer.

11. He lost a great deal of political support because his speeches were so full of **uncertainty** and anomalies.

> *Don't forget to keep a record of the words and expressions that you have learnt, review your notes from time to time and try to use new vocabulary items whenever possible.*

© Peter Collin Publishing 2001. For reference see *English Dictionary for Students* (1-901659-06-2)

# Unit Nine

## 9e - Choose the best word

**For each of the sentences here, choose the best word from *a, b or c*.**

1. There are still too many countries which regularly _____ their citizens' human rights.

   **a. break**            **b. violate**            **c. breach**

2. In very hot climates, a considerable amount of petrol _____ from car fuel tanks and into the atmosphere.

   **a. evaporates**       **b. dehydrates**         **c. dries**

3. When writing a summary, try to _____ the main ideas into just a few short sentences.

   **a. condense**         **b. shrink**             **c. collapse**

4. The chief _____ which many companies have today is not the property they own but rather the creativity and skills of their employees.

   **a. asset**            **b. benefit**            **c. liability**

5. His health is so bad that it will be a _____ if he is alive next year.

   **a. wonder**           **b. miracle**            **c. marvel**

6. When you hit a drum, the movement of the drum causes the air molecules to _____ , which we hear as sound.

   **a. reverberate**      **b. vibrate**            **c. shake**

7. Although the research team are all somewhat _____ people, they work very well together and produce some very good ideas.

   **a. conventional**     **b. odd**                **c. bizarre**

8. The professor _____ several possible explanations for the rise in recorded crime.

   **a. numbered**         **b. enumerated**         **c. named**

9. The supervisor was not _____ concerned about the student asking for a week's extension to finish his essay, but warned him that there would be no more extensions after that.

   **a. unduly**           **b. absolutely**         **c. highly**

10. Please _____ two colour passport photographs to the application form.

    **a. link**            **b. attach**             **c. fix**

> *Don't forget to keep a record of the words and expressions that you have learnt, review your notes from time to time and try to use new vocabulary items whenever possible.*

© Peter Collin Publishing 2001. For reference see *English Dictionary for Students* (1-901659-06-2)

## 9f - Make a collocation

Start by reading through the sentences below. Then take one word from the box on the left and combine this with one from the box on the right to make a collocation. (Note that more than one pairing may be possible and also that some words appear more than once.) Then try to match your combinations with the spaces in the sentences below:

---

| |
|---|
| full • frontiers • drastic • rural |
| high • gained • voluntary • wide |
| umbilical • low • federal |

| |
|---|
| of science • work • areas • action |
| cord • morale • momentum • velocity |
| complement • vocabulary • government |

1. In the United States, the _____ _____ has overall responsibility for foreign affairs and defence.

2. The company was losing so much money that only _____ _____ by the management — including the dismissal of 15% of the employees — enabled it to survive.

3. Until very recently, most people lived and worked in _____ _____ , whereas today most of us live in cities.

4. Young children need a stimulating environment so that they can develop the _____ _____ of intellectual and social skills.

5. Researchers work at the _____ _____ in order to increase our knowledge.

6. While walking in space, the astronauts are connected to the spacecraft by a long life-line, often referred to as the _____ _____ .

7. After retiring, many people choose to do some type of _____ _____ even though they receive no pay for this.

8. Political change in Central Europe _____ _____ when President Gorbachev came to power in the Soviet Union.

9. All students will need a _____ _____ in order to understand the sources of information they have to use.

10. Policemen carrying _____ _____ rifles surrounded the building.

11. If soldiers are not paid on time, _____ _____ can set in, sometimes resulting in a revolution against the government.

---

*Don't forget to keep a record of the words and expressions that you have learnt, review your notes from time to time and try to use new vocabulary items whenever possible.*

© Peter Collin Publishing 2001. For reference see *English Dictionary for Students* (1-901659-06-2)

# Unit Nine

## Vocabulary sheet

Don't forget to keep a record of the words and expressions that you have learnt, review your notes from time to time and try to use new vocabulary items whenever possible.

© Peter Collin Publishing 2001. For reference see *English Dictionary for Students* (1-901659-06-2)

# Unit Ten

## 10a - Fill in the gaps

**From the following list, use each word only once to complete the sentences below. Remember that in the case of nouns and verbs you may need to change the form of the word:**

---

anthropology (n) • foetus (n) • intimacy (n) • province (n) • quote (v)

render (v) • repress (v) • sift (v) • surplus (n) • triangle (n)

---

1.  The costs were so enormous that they _____ the project impossible.

2.  _____ is the scientific study of man including such topics as religion and culture.

3.  One of the simplest but strongest shapes is the _____ .

4.  The _____ between a mother and a child is very important for the emotional development of the child.

5.  If you have made a plan for your writing, it becomes much easier to _____ through your notes and decide which ideas to include.

6.  When there is a _____ of oil, the price on the world market falls.

7.  In nearly all parts of Eastern Europe, attempts to _____ movements for political change failed completely.

8.  The Canadian capital Ottawa is in the _____ of Ontario.

9.  Recent research has shown that drinking heavily during pregnancy can harm the _____ .

10. When you want to _____ something, make sure that the words you write are exactly the same as those in your source.

---

## 10b - Choose the right word

**In each of the sentences below, decide which of the words in *bold* is more suitable:**

---

1.  Although many drugs are illegal, it appears to be increasingly easy for teenagers to ***procure/secure*** drugs if they want them.

2.  If you have a lot of data which you want to include, an ***appendix/index*** at the end of the report or essay is the best place for it.

© Peter Collin Publishing 2001. For reference see *English Dictionary for Students* (1-901659-06-2)

# Unit Ten

3. Before they take their examinations, students should revise thoroughly and try to *assimilate/ingest* what they have been studying.

4. A huge trench was dug to *channel/deviate* excess water away from farming areas.

5. According to opponents of the death penalty, the idea that executions help to prevent murder is a complete *myth/legend.*

6. For health reasons, smoking is restricted if not completely *embargoed/prohibited* in many public places.

7. At the end of an essay, students should always *append/affix* a bibliography, giving details of the sources of information they have used.

8. France's road and rail networks *diverge/converge* on Paris because it is the capital.

9. The influence of television is so great that actors can be *elevated/lifted* to superstar status almost overnight.

10. Some years ago, the shapes of cars were very *angular/bent* whereas today they are much more rounded.

## 10c - Finish the sentence

**Choose the best ending for each of the sentence extracts below from the list underneath:**

1. Many people working today find it difficult to *tolerate*...
2. In Canada, it is a huge advantage to be *fluent*...
3. Although the lecturer's explanation was very *cogent*,...
4. In some American states, there is a strange *anomaly*...
5. In recent years, some Asian countries have *emerged*...
6. Some analysts think that many customers will *dispense*...
7. New government proposals will increase the *rigour*...
8. University students usually have the *option*...
9. A new drug developed by a leading company *purports*...
10. Although it was particularly radical and *ingenious*,...
11. Sometimes articles are *anonymous*,...

a. ...whereby a 16 year-old may get married but is not allowed to buy a beer.
b. ...but in the majority of cases the name of the author appears with the article.
c. ...some students still could not understand the solution to the problem.
d. ...with conventional phones altogether and use mobile phones instead.
e. ...of choosing extra subjects to study if they wish.
f. ...from almost nothing to become major economic players.
g. ...in both French and English.
h. ...the design for the Concorde was just too expensive to produce commercially.
i. ...high levels of stress and insecurity.
j. ...of the law by introducing longer prison sentences.
k. ...to slow down the ageing process.

© Peter Collin Publishing 2001. For reference see *English Dictionary for Students* (1-901659-06-2)

## 10d - Word substitution

From the list below, choose one word which could be used in place of the language shown in *bold* without changing the meaning of the sentence. Remember that you may need to change the form or in some cases the grammatical class of the word:

> ascribe (v) • assent (n) • comprise (v) • emancipate (v) • embrace (v) • enhance (v)
>
> inconsistent (adj) • interrelate (v) • outcome (n) • saturate (v) • vague (adj)

1.  The minister resigned because many people felt that his behaviour was *at variance* with his role in public life.
2.  The clear increase in skin cancer has been *attributed* to the fact that more people now take holidays in hot countries.
3.  The new law course attempts to *cover* all aspects of international law.
4.  Some people argue that robots in the home will *liberate* us from having to do the housework in the not too distant future.
5.  A significant number of students decide to study for a Master's degree to *boost* their knowledge.
6.  The USA *is composed of* 52 states.
7.  In Britain, the Queen must give her *agreement* to a new law before it can come into force.
8.  The *result* of the experiment was a complete surprise to everyone: the new process was a success!
9.  The market for cars in Europe is almost *full to capacity,* forcing car manufacturers to look for customers elsewhere.
10. A recent survey has found that most people have only an *uncertain* understanding of how and why we study theoretical science.
11. Wages and inflation are closely *linked,* in that as one rises or falls so does the other.

## 10e - Choose the best word

For each of the sentences here, choose the best word from *a, b* or *c*:

1.  The President's speech was so _____ that many people were persuaded to accept the need for change.
    *a. expressive*          *b. articulate*          *c. eloquent*
2.  Car crashes are almost always accidental, but on rare occasions they may be _____ .
    *a. conscious*          *b. purposeful*          *c. deliberate*
3.  The outline is a kind of _____ which gives in general terms the basic structure and content of a piece of work.
    *a. sketch*          *b. skeleton*          *c. draft*
4.  People who smoke heavily experience a/an_____ to smoke, which makes it very difficult for them to stop.
    *a. compulsion*          *b. obligation*          *c. addiction*
5.  Although we now believe this to be impossible, early scientists tried to produce _____ motion machines, that is, machines which would never stop.
    *a. perpetual*          *b. everlasting*          *c. undying*
6.  If a questionnaire is badly written, it will not _____ the type of information required from the people completing it.
    *a. solicit*          *b. elicit*          *c. obtain*

© Peter Collin Publishing 2001. For reference see *English Dictionary for Students* (1-901659-06-2)

# Unit Ten

7. Books are usually electronically protected so that they cannot be _____ from the library unless they have been issued in the proper way.
   a. removed      b. withdrawn      c. extracted

8. Studying is important, but playing sports and joining clubs will help to _____ a student's time at university.
   a. boost      b. enrich      c. bolster

9. No doubt every country has _____ in its history which its people now regret.
   a. episodes      b. stages      c. sections

10. Students who are _____ on the campus make more use of the university sports facilities than those living outside.
    a. domiciled      b. resident      c. settled

11. One of the biggest problems with malaria is that the disease can _____ and give the patient serious medical complications again and again throughout his or her life.
    a. repeat      b. recur      c. arise

# 10f - Make a collocation

**Start by reading through the sentences below. Then take one word from the box on the left and combine this with one from the box on the right to make a collocation. (Note that more than one pairing may be possible and also that some words appear more than once.) Then try to match your combinations with the spaces in the sentences below:**

| | |
|---|---|
| maternal • television • high • have<br><br>political • health • leading • fossil<br><br>null and • tangible • under | interviews • instinct • void • inflation<br><br>clinic • ambitions • benefits • fuels<br><br>the auspices of • exponents • access to |

1. In many universities, there is a/an _____ _____ provided especially for students and staff.

2. _____ _____ is usually an economic disaster, causing prices to rise and the value of money to fall.

3. In _____ _____ , politicians often ignore what they are asked, preferring instead to discuss their own interests.

4. Because they increase the availability of information, _____ _____ of computer technology argue that computers help protect our freedom.

5. Many feminists now argue that women do not have a _____ _____ towards children.

6. Many successful business figures want to enter government in order to satisfy their _____ _____ .

7. Because the original information was incorrect, the court decided that the contract was _____ _____ .

8. The building of a new airport will bring _____ _____ , such as improved communications and more jobs in the local area.

9. Through the Internet, students now _____ _____ information from academic libraries all over the world.

10. One of the problems with _____ _____ such as coal and oil is that they will not last for ever.

11. An international rescue operation was organised _____ _____ the United Nations.

© Peter Collin Publishing 2001. For reference see *English Dictionary for Students* (1-901659-06-2)

## Vocabulary sheet

---

---

---

---

---

---

---

---

---

---

---

---

---

---

---

---

---

---

---

---

---

---

---

---

---

---

---

*Don't forget to keep a record of the words and expressions that you have learnt, review your notes from time to time and try to use new vocabulary items whenever possible.*

© Peter Collin Publishing 2001. For reference see *English Dictionary for Students* (1-901659-06-2)

# Unit Eleven

## 11a - Fill in the gaps

From the following list, use each word only once to complete the sentences below.
Remember that in the case of nouns and verbs you may need to change the form of the word:

---

challenge   (n)   •   diameter   (n)   •   enable   (v)   •   expert   (n)

export   (n)   •   fundamental   (adj)   •   import   (n)   •   luxury   (n)

pest   (n)   •   pollution   (n)   •   starve   (v)   •   temporary   (adj)   •   tractor   (n)

---

1.  The _____ of live animals is strictly controlled so as to prevent diseases from being brought into the country.

2.  We recommend that you take a pre-sessional study skills course, which will _____ you to practise the language skills you will need later.

3.  Supplying _____ to Third World farmers may seem an excellent idea, but in practice these machines are often not suited to local conditions and so tend to break down.

4.  Some business leaders become bored with well-established organisations and prefer instead the _____ of setting up a new company.

5.  During the 1980's, thousands of people _____ in Sudan and Ethiopia because there was no food.

6.  The USA has a huge domestic market and so is less reliant on _____ for the success of its economy.

7.  One major problem with some early insecticides was that they tended to kill not only harmful _____ but also those insects which actually helped the farmer.

8.  Most international students choose to live in university accommodation, while others may stay with a host family as a _____ measure before renting their own houses.

9.  In many developed countries, what used to be considered as _____ goods are now regarded as necessities.

10. Jupiter is the largest planet in our solar system, with a _____ of about 570,000 kilometres.

11. With any quotation you wish to use, make sure that the author you are quoting is an _____ or academic authority.

12. Increasingly, major industrial companies are finding that consumers are concerned about any _____ created by the manufacture of their products.

13. The Director reminded the middle managers that full cooperation from all workers was _____ to the success of the company.

© Peter Collin Publishing 2001. For reference see English Dictionary for Students (1-901659-06-2)

## 11b - Choose the right word

In each of the sentences below, decide which of the words in *bold* is more suitable:

1.  Two of the missing children have been rescued but the *fate/destiny* of the other six is still unknown.

2.  The *process/action* by which plants use sunlight to produce food is known as photosynthesis.

3.  Very small *bubbles/blobs* of air can become trapped in liquid metal, causing it to become weak.

4.  At first, students were *hostile/unfriendly* to the idea of being videoed during their presentations, but they soon realised that this would help them to improve their technique.

5.  The government lost the election because of a whole *brochure/catalogue* of scandals and political errors.

6.  Following the decision to pass legislation to *compel/urge* employers to improve safety standards at work, the number of deaths from accidents has fallen sharply.

7.  Car *theft/burglary* remains higher in Britain than in any other European country.

8.  In the past, large parts of Holland were *drained/emptied* of water to produce new farmland.

9.  The area around the Great Pyramids is one of the most important archeological *sites/spots* for the study of ancient Egypt.

10. Until recently, goods from countries such as Taiwan and Korea were often thought to be *worse/inferior,* and yet today these countries make many high-quality products.

11. The introduction of the fax and more recently e-mail has made it much easier to *communicate/contact* with other people all around the world.

---

*Don't forget to keep a record of the words and expressions that you have learnt, review your notes from time to time and try to use new vocabulary items whenever possible.*

---

**67**

© Peter Collin Publishing 2001. For reference see *English Dictionary for Students* (1-901659-06-2)

# Unit Eleven

## 11c - Finish the sentence

Choose the best ending for each of the sentence extracts below from the list underneath:

1. According to a recent large-scale government *survey*...

2. Car manufacturers are keen to develop other sources of *fuel*...

3. An increase in the number of accidents led to a public *debate*...

4. Although it means that people live longer, the *equipment*...

5. Japan's greatest *resource*...

6. A group of students decided to complain because one tutor *cancelled*...

7. Some countries use a thirteen-month *calendar*...

8. Young plants will grow quickly if the soil is *moist*...

9. Increasingly, universities are being asked to *undertake*...

10. As people can now make purchases on *impulse*...

11. Computers make use of the binary system (0,1), unlike the *decimal*...

12. Although the new equipment performed well under *laboratory*...

---

a. ...based on the lunar cycle, rather than the more normal twelve-month system.

b. ...about the safety of the national railway system.

c. ...system (0-9) which we use in everyday life.

d. ...used in modern hospitals has increased the cost of health care.

e. ... — such as solar power — since oil will not last for ever.

f. ...with credit cards, buying habits have changed.

g. ...all tutorials for a week.

h. ...conditions, it was simply not robust enough for everyday use.

i. ...and warm, but not if it is too damp or cold.

j. ...is its people, since it has very few sources of raw materials or energy.

k. ...conducted in the UK, levels of reading and writing skills are still low.

l. ...research in order to develop new products on behalf of large companies.

> *Don't forget to keep a record of the words and expressions that you have learnt, review your notes from time to time and try to use new vocabulary items whenever possible.*

© Peter Collin Publishing 2001. For reference see *English Dictionary for Students* (1-901659-06-2)

## 11d - Word substitution

From the list below, choose one word which could be used in place of the language shown in *bold* without changing the meaning of the sentence. Remember that you may need to change the form or in some cases the grammatical class of the word:

| | | | |
|---|---|---|---|
| bulk (n) • | fluid (n) • | fulfil (v) • | huge (adj) |
| inspect (v) • | instance (n) • | novel (n) • | revolve (v) |
| shrink (v) • | switch (v) • | topic (n) • | vital (adj) |

1.  In some *cases*, the patients did not make any improvement, but generally the treatment was a huge success.

2.  While a few students stay in university halls of residence, the *majority* of students choose to rent their own accommodation at some point in their studies.

3.  In the course of a marathon, a runner needs to drink water periodically in order to make up for the *liquid* lost through sweating.

4.  Before starting work on your dissertation, make sure that you have discussed the *subject* with your supervisor.

5.  Staff responsible for *examining* aircraft checked the plane and declared it unsafe.

6.  Some students find it very confusing when a lecturer *changes* from the topic under discussion to share a joke with his audience.

7.  The *stories* of Charles Dickens give us a very clear picture of life in Britain in the nineteenth century.

8.  Many students complained when the university failed to *keep* its promise to allow students 24 hour access to the computer centre.

9.  Each time the star *rotates,* it sends out a radio signal which we can detect on Earth, allowing us to calculate the speed of rotation.

10. It is absolutely *essential* that you check your examination entries to make sure they are correct; if they are not you may not be allowed to sit your examination.

11. Most universities have found that demand for engineering courses has *decreased,* while new subjects such as media studies have become very popular.

12. The amount of money owed by some Third World countries is so *enormous* that it will probably never be repaid.

© Peter Collin Publishing 2001. For reference see *English Dictionary for Students* (1-901659-06-2)

# Unit Eleven

## 11e - Choose the best word

For each of the sentences here, choose the best word from *a, b* or *c*.

1.  In addition to reading books and journals, the other main source of information available to university students is the _____ given by the academic staff.

    **a. lectures**              **b. lessons**              **c. classes**

2.  The atmospheres of most planets is not _____ , making it difficult for us to see the surface.

    **a. transparent**           **b. lucid**                **c. clear**

3.  Three terrorists managed to escape but all of them were _____ within 24 hours and returned to prison.

    **a. trapped**               **b. snared**               **c. captured**

4.  Anybody who joins the army as a soldier has to accept that danger is an _____ part of the job.

    **a. inside**                **b. internal**             **c. inherent**

5.  Students without the normal academic qualifications but who have relevant work experience may be offered a place on an easier diploma course on the _____ towards an MBA.

    **a. journey**               **b. direction**            **c. route**

6.  In Egypt, water from the River Nile has been used for thousands of years to _____ the dry desert land so that crops may be grown.

    **a. irrigate**              **b. moisten**              **c. fundamental**

7.  Improvements in quality control techniques have resulted in more high-quality products with very few _____ .

    **a. mistakes**              **b. failures**             **c. defects**

8.  As you can see from your handout, the first _____ of figures down the left-hand side shows the growth in population.

    **a. line**                  **b. column**               **c. string**

9.  The _____ of men to women in China is unusual, in that there are more men then women.

    **a. ratio**                 **b. number**               **c. quantity**

10. According to a recent survey in Europe, most workers expressed a preference for increased _____ time rather than the chance to do more overtime and earn extra money.

    **a. leisure**               **b. hobby**                **c. relaxation**

---

*Don't forget to keep a record of the words and expressions that you have learnt, review your notes from time to time and try to use new vocabulary items whenever possible.*

© Peter Collin Publishing 2001. For reference see *English Dictionary for Students* (1-901659-06-2)

## 11f - Make a collocation

**Start by reading through the sentences below. Then take one word from the box on the left and combine this with one from the box on the right to make a collocation. (Note that more than one pairing may be possible and also that some words appear more than once.) Then try to match your combinations with the spaces in the sentences below:**

| | |
|---|---|
| public • television • tropical<br><br>cassette • electrical • mental<br><br>air • gas • academic • career | circuits • illness • stations<br><br>rain forests • change • tapes • fares<br><br>cylinders • journals • transport |

1.  In modern cars, sound systems play CDs rather than _____ _____ .

2.  The _____ _____ of the Amazon contain over 10% of all known plant species found on Earth.

3.  One of the most important developments in the history of the computer was the printing of tiny _____ _____ on small chips of silicon.

4.  The explosion was caused by terrorists, who had packed a number of _____ _____ with home-made explosive.

5.  Increasingly, cars are being excluded from city centres and improved _____ _____ is being developed instead.

6.  For the most recent research developments in any subject, _____ _____ are a much better place to look in than text-books.

7.  Psychologists have shown that living in very tall buildings can lead to depression, or even _____ _____ .

8.  Thanks to the introduction of satellite communications, we can confidently expect the growth in the number of _____ _____ to continue.

9.  An increase in competition among the airlines in Europe should mean that _____ _____ will become much cheaper.

10. After several years working as a lawyer, she decided to have a _____ _____ and become a university lecturer instead.

*Don't forget to keep a record of the words and expressions that you have learnt, review your notes from time to time and try to use new vocabulary items whenever possible.*

© Peter Collin Publishing 2001. For reference see *English Dictionary for Students* (1-901659-06-2)

# Unit Eleven

## Vocabulary sheet

_____

_____

_____

_____

_____

_____

_____

_____

_____

_____

_____

_____

_____

_____

_____

_____

_____

_____

_____

_____

_____

_____

_____

_____

_____

_____

_____

*Don't forget to keep a record of the words and expressions that you have learnt, review your notes from time to time and try to use new vocabulary items whenever possible.*

© Peter Collin Publishing 2001. For reference see *English Dictionary for Students* (1-901659-06-2)

## Unit One

**1a**

| | | | | |
|---|---|---|---|---|
| 1. similar | 2. formulate | 3. context | 4. devised | 5. vertical |
| 6. impact | 7. usage | 8. summary | 9. denote | 10. arbitrary |
| 11. assigned | 12. criteria | 13. ignored | 14. data | |

**1b**

| | | | | |
|---|---|---|---|---|
| 1. evident | 2. publishes | 3. involving | 4. negative | 5. environment |
| 6. evaluate | 7. range | 8. modified | 9. restricted | 10. derive |
| 11. varies | 12. pursued | 13. consists of | | |

**1c**

| | | | | |
|---|---|---|---|---|
| 1. m | 2. c | 3. a | 4. h | 5. b |
| 6. g | 7. j | 8. e | 9. l | 10. k |
| 11. i | 12. d | 13. f | | |

**1d**

| | | | | |
|---|---|---|---|---|
| 1. comply with | 2. equivalent | 3. specify | 4. is required | 5. obvious |
| 6. presuming | 7. guarantee | 8. methods | 9. imply | 10. sum |
| 11. proceeding | 12. concluded | | | |

**1e**

| | | | | |
|---|---|---|---|---|
| 1. assess | 2. dominate | 3. definite | 4. approach | 5. potential |
| 6. elements | 7. components | 8. compensate | 9. subsequent | 10. distinct |
| 11. indicates | 12. regions | 13. prime | | |

**1f**

| | | |
|---|---|---|
| 1. valid reason | 2. new concept | 3. constant temperature |
| 4. new dimension | 5. analyse results | 6. establish a link |
| 7. tense atmosphere | 8. initial results | 9. leading role |
| 10. ultimate responsibility | 11. marital status | 12. put forward a hypothesis |
| 13. reverse the verdict | 14. minimum requirement | |

## Unit Two

**2a**

| | | | | |
|---|---|---|---|---|
| 1. manipulate | 2. creating | 3. conceived | 4. ensued | 5. innovative |
| 6. automatic | 7. mathematics | 8. achieving | 9. period | 10. equilibrium |
| 11. tradition | 12. series | 13. preceded | 14. sections | 15. stable |

**2b**

| | | | | |
|---|---|---|---|---|
| 1. occurs | 2. passive | 3. respective | 4. infer | 5. accelerating |
| 6. major | 7. portion | 8. fluctuate | 9. contribute | 10. focus |
| 11. design | 12. convert | 13. comprehend | 14. authorise | |

**2c**

| | | | | |
|---|---|---|---|---|
| 1. h | 2. d | 3. k | 4. f | 5. a |
| 6. l | 7. c | 8. j | 9. b | 10. m |
| 11. e | 12. n | 13. g | 14. l | 15. o |

**2d**

| | | | | |
|---|---|---|---|---|
| 1. decade | 2. emphasize | 3. expose | 4. structure | 5. signified |
| 6. generated | 7. consequent | 8. capillaries | 9. notion | 10. affects |
| 11. predict | 12. pertinent | 13. undergone | 14. select | |

**2e**

| | | | | |
|---|---|---|---|---|
| 1. external | 2. contrast | 3. simultaneous | 4. chapters | 5. approximate |
| 6. technology | 7. verify | 8. phase | 9. principle | 10. obtained |
| 11. magnetic | 12. segments | 13. individual | 14. empirical | |

© Peter Collin Publishing 2001. For reference see *English Dictionary for Students* (1-901659-06-2)

# Answers

**2f**

1. natural phenomena
2. highly sophisticated
3. sequence of events
4. reacted angrily
5. economically feasible
6. endangered species
7. assert the right
8. verbal agreement
9. precise details
10. devote time and money
11. inhibit growth
12. transmit signals
13. separate entities

## Unit Three

**3a**

| | | | | |
|---|---|---|---|---|
| 1. norm | 2. discrete | 3. co-ordinate | 4. geography | 5. sources |
| 6. preposition | 7. estimates | 8. underlying | 9. rational | 10. pole |
| 11. scheme | 12. task | | | |

**3b**

| | | | | |
|---|---|---|---|---|
| 1. deficient | 2. plot | 3. transition | 4. appropriate | 5. proprietor |
| 6. communes | 7. convened | 8. satellites | 9. issue | 10. deviate |
| 11. factor | 12. abandoned | | | |

**3c**

| | | | | |
|---|---|---|---|---|
| 1. c | 2. j | 3. f | 4. d | 5. l |
| 6. g | 7. e | 8. k | 9. i | 10. h |
| 11. b | 12. a | | | |

**3d**

| | | | | |
|---|---|---|---|---|
| 1. dispose of | 2. chemicals | 3. credible | 4. rely on | 5. adequate |
| 6. consume | 7. accomplished | 8. occupied | 9. exerts | 10. manifested |
| 11. conduct | 12. areas | | | |

**3e**

| | | | | |
|---|---|---|---|---|
| 1. adjust | 2. superficial | 3. maximum | 4. circumstances | 5. revealed |
| 6. image | 7. drama | 8. motive | 9. orientate | 10. explicit |
| 11. contaminated | 12. contact | 13. appreciate | | |

**3f**

1. labour shortage
2. dynamic personality
3. physical exercise
4. power and prestige
5. final decision
6. classic example
7. previous experience
8. positive aspects
9. outspoken critic
10. common feature
11. computer network
12. global economy

## Unit Four

**4a**

| | | | | |
|---|---|---|---|---|
| 1. impressed | 2. distributed | 3. analogy | 4. energy | 5. perpendicular |
| 6. speculate | 7. text | 8. administer | 9. rejected | 10. spontaneous |
| 11. assembled | 12. intervene | | | |

**4b**

| | | | | |
|---|---|---|---|---|
| 1. sphere | 2. psychology | 3. investigate | 4. axis | 5. appraises |
| 6. symbols | 7. heredity | 8. discourse | 9. acquire | 10. tentative |
| 11. emotion | | | | |

**4c**

| | | | | |
|---|---|---|---|---|
| 1. d | 2. k | 3. e | 4. a | 5. l |
| 6. j | 7. f | 8. b | 9. i | 10. c |
| 11. g | 12. h | | | |

**4d**

| | | | | |
|---|---|---|---|---|
| 1. alleged | 2. ceased | 3. elaborate | 4. alter | 5. fragment |
| 6. philosophy | 7. upsurge | 8 subsided | 9. induced | 10. reservoir |
| 11. litigation | | | | |

© Peter Collin Publishing 2001. For reference see *English Dictionary for Students* (1-901659-06-2)

**4e**

| | | | | |
|---|---|---|---|---|
| 1. superimpose | 2. atoms | 3. revolt | 4. attributed to | 5. research |
| 6. project | 7. internal | 8. eliminated | 9. logic | 10. goal |
| 11. integrate | 12. constitute | | | |

**4f**

| | | |
|---|---|---|
| 1. flatly contradicted | 2. atom bombs | 3. high proportion |
| 4. Western culture | 5. judicial system | 6. dedicated his life |
| 7. dense fog | 8. embodies the principle | 9. mobile phones |
| 10. military service | | |

# Unit Five

**5a**

| | | | | |
|---|---|---|---|---|
| 1. X-rays | 2. edit | 3. version | 4. trivial | 5. homogeneous |
| 6. stress | 7. aid | 8. symptom | 9. traits | 10. overlapped |
| 11. biology | 12. enlighten | | | |

**5b**

| | | | | |
|---|---|---|---|---|
| 1. absorb | 2. contrary | 3. secure | 4. respond | 5. categories |
| 6. objective | 7. stimulated | 8. implement | 9. suppress | 10. duration |
| 11. expel | 12. transformed | | | |

**5c**

| | | | | |
|---|---|---|---|---|
| 1. f | 2. g | 3. e | 4. c | 5. h |
| 6. l | 7. a | 8. b | 9. i | 10. j |
| 11. k | 12. d | | | |

**5d**

| | | | | |
|---|---|---|---|---|
| 1. advocate | 2. contract | 3. preliminary | 4. tiny | 5. graph |
| 6. transferred | 7. dictates | 8. subtle | 9. retard | 10. compound |
| 11. insisted | | | | |

**5e**

| | | | | |
|---|---|---|---|---|
| 1. disputes | 2. execute | 3. restore | 4. supplement | 5. confronted |
| 6. diffuse | 7. superior | 8. rudimentary | 9. instruct | 10. label |
| 11. client | 12. fraud | | | |

**5f**

| | | |
|---|---|---|
| 1. at regular intervals | 2. abstract thought | 3. force of gravity |
| 4. crisis of confidence | 5. legitimate concern | 6. within a radius |
| 7. err on the side of caution | 8. lines intersect | 9. imposed a ban |
| 10. research institutes | 11. perpetrated crimes | |

# Unit Six

**6a**

| | | | | |
|---|---|---|---|---|
| 1. academic | 2. metabolism | 3. strata | 4. aroused | 5. interlocking |
| 6. hierarchy | 7. radical | 8. compute | 9. benefits | 10. degenerated |
| 11. instinct | 12. contend | | | |

**6b**

| | | | | |
|---|---|---|---|---|
| 1. protest | 2. interact | 3. Medium- | 4. abnormal | 5. participated |
| 6. oblige | 7. decline | 8. tone | 9. commit | 10. terminology |
| 11. awe | 12. appeal | | | |

**6c**

| | | | | |
|---|---|---|---|---|
| 1. e | 2. b | 3. d | 4. f | 5. c |
| 6. a | 7. h | 8. i | 9. g | 10. k |
| 11. l | 12. m | 13. j | | |

© Peter Collin Publishing 2001. For reference see *English Dictionary for Students* (1-901659-06-2)

# Answers

answers

**6d**

| | | | | |
|---|---|---|---|---|
| 1. clarify | 2. propagate | 3. converse | 4. inclined | 5. assist |
| 6. extracts | 7. sustain | 8. urban | 9. propensity | 10. demonstrated |

**6e**

| | | | | |
|---|---|---|---|---|
| 1. legal | 2. revise | 3. an adult | 4. collided | 5. comment |
| 6. assured | 7. prospered | 8. income | 9. locate | 10 fertile |
| 11. console | 12. volume | 13. cooperate | | |

**6f**

| | | |
|---|---|---|
| 1. keep your nerve | 2. economic sanctions | 3. endless cycle |
| 4. attain their goals | 5. go off at a tangent | 6. identical twins |
| 7. virtual reality | 8. under the microscope | 9. southern hemisphere |
| 10. brief interlude | 11. niche market | |

## Unit Seven

**7a**

| | | | | |
|---|---|---|---|---|
| 1. cells | 2. adolescents | 3. collapsed | 4. friction | 5. commodity |
| 6. affiliate | 7. muscle | 8. dissolve | 9. repudiated | 10. saint |
| 11. aristocracy | 12. democracy | 13. invoke | | |

**7b**

| | | | | |
|---|---|---|---|---|
| 1. depressed | 2. obsolete | 3. odour | 4. refute | 5. texture |
| 6. pragmatic | 7. incessant | 8. scores | 9. creditors | 10. confer |
| 11. policy | 12. migrate | 13. configuration | | |

**7c**

| | | | | |
|---|---|---|---|---|
| 1. b | 2. g | 3. e | 4. f | 5. l |
| 6. c | 7. a | 8. j | 9. i | 10. k |
| 11. d | 12. h | | | |

**7d**

| | | | | |
|---|---|---|---|---|
| 1. rhythm | 2. domestic | 3. conserve | 4. defer | 5. incentives |
| 6. corporate | 7. fraction | 8. horror | 9. alcohol | 10. prudence |
| 11. negotiate | 12. competence | 13. peasants | | |

**7e**

| | | | | |
|---|---|---|---|---|
| 1. Finance | 2. reform | 3. continent | 4. tissue | 5. stereotype |
| 6. astronomy | 7. neutral | 8. nutrients | 9. transact | 10. schedule |
| 11. degrade | 12. rectangle | | | |

**7f**

| | | |
|---|---|---|
| 1. precipitated a crisis | 2. thermal energy | 3. salt crystals |
| 4. pleaded not guilty | 5. a code of ethics | 6. Sibling rivalry |
| 7. intermediate stages | 8. political spectrum | 9. campaign of terror |
| 10. colloquial language | 11. contingent upon | 12. US Congress |

## Unit Eight

**8a**

| | | | | |
|---|---|---|---|---|
| 1. lenses | 2. liable | 3. aggregate | 4. pendulum | 5. Supreme |
| 6. Nuclear | 7. fraternal | 8. subordinate | 9. oxygen | 10. reproduce |
| 11. postulated | | | | |

**8b**

| | | | | |
|---|---|---|---|---|
| 1. allies | 2. adhere | 3. metaphor | 4. coincided | 5. pervaded |
| 6. reluctant | 7. index | 8. detriment | 9. fallacy | 10. trend |
| 11. finite | | | | |

© Peter Collin Publishing 2001. For reference see *English Dictionary for Students* (1-901659-06-2)

8c

| | | | | |
|---|---|---|---|---|
| 1. f | 2. b | 3. e | 4. k | 5. i |
| 6. a | 7. c | 8. d | 9. j | 10. h |
| 11. g | | | | |

8d

| | | | | |
|---|---|---|---|---|
| 1. evolved | 2. proclaimed | 3. cater | 4. testify | 5. drugs |
| 6. utilise | 7. discern | 8. territory | 9. allude | 10. launch |
| 11. Rebels | | | | |

8e

| | | | | |
|---|---|---|---|---|
| 1. exude | 2. allocates | 3. deprived | 4. provoked | 5. frustrated |
| 6. circulates | 7. league | 8. magic | 9. currency | 10. partisan |

8f

| | | |
|---|---|---|
| 1. sex and violence | 2. dissipates energy | 3. Peace Treaty |
| 4. solar power | 5. legislate against | 6. utter waste of time |
| 7. imperial control | 8. on the premise that | 9. invest money |
| 10. give their consent | | |

## Unit Nine

9a

| | | | | |
|---|---|---|---|---|
| 1. carbon | 2. Prince | 3. integers | 4. lustre | 5. molecule |
| 6. breed | 7. illuminated | 8. stationary | 9. batteries | 10. acid |
| 11. matrix | | | | |

9b

| | | | | |
|---|---|---|---|---|
| 1. fund | 2. exhaust | 3. mistress | 4. penal | 5. liberated |
| 6. evoke | 7. diverge | 8. torture | 9. intrinsic | 10. accumulated |

9c

| | | | | |
|---|---|---|---|---|
| 1. i | 2. h | 3. e | 4. f | 5. k |
| 6. d | 7. b | 8. j | 9. a | 10. g |
| 11. c | | | | |

9d

| | | | | |
|---|---|---|---|---|
| 1. annual | 2. efficient | 3. construed | 4. innate | 5. suspended |
| 6. material | 7. orbits | 8. reverberated | 9. residue | 10. displace |
| 11. ambiguity | | | | |

9e

| | | | | |
|---|---|---|---|---|
| 1. violate | 2. evaporates | 3. condense | 4. asset | 5. miracle |
| 6. vibrate | 7. odd | 8. enumerated | 9. unduly | 10. attach |

9f

| | | |
|---|---|---|
| 1. Federal Government | 2. drastic action | 3. rural areas |
| 4. full complement | 5. frontiers of science | 6. umbilical cord |
| 7. voluntary work | 8. gained momentum | 9. wide vocabulary |
| 10. high velocity | 11. low morale | |

## Unit Ten

10a

| | | | | |
|---|---|---|---|---|
| 1. rendered | 2. Anthropology | 3. triangle | 4. intimacy | 5. sift |
| 6. surplus | 7. repress | 8. province | 9. foetus | 10. quote |

10b

| | | | | |
|---|---|---|---|---|
| 1. procure | 2. appendix | 3. assimilate | 4. channel | 5. myth |
| 6. prohibited | 7. append | 8. converge | 9. elevated | 10. angular |

**77**

© Peter Collin Publishing 2001. For reference see *English Dictionary for Students* (1-901659-06-2)

# Answers

### 10c

| | | | | |
|---|---|---|---|---|
| 1. i | 2. g | 3. c | 4. a | 5. f |
| 6. d | 7. j | 8. e | 9. k | 10. h |
| 11. b | | | | |

### 10d

| | | | | |
|---|---|---|---|---|
| 1. inconsistent | 2. ascribed | 3. embrace | 4. emancipate | 5. enhance |
| 6. comprises | 7. assent | 8. outcome | 9. saturated | 10. vague |
| 11. interrelated | | | | |

### 10e

| | | | | |
|---|---|---|---|---|
| 1. eloquent | 2. deliberate | 3. sketch | 4. compulsion | 5. perpetual |
| 6. elicit | 7. removed | 8. enrich | 9. episodes | 10. resident |
| 11. recur | | | | |

### 10f

| | | |
|---|---|---|
| 1. health clinic | 2. High inflation | 3. television interviews |
| 4. leading exponents | 5. maternal instinct | 6. political ambitions |
| 7. null and void | 8. tangible benefits | 9. have access to |
| 10. fossil fuels | 11. under the auspices of | |

## Unit Eleven

### 11a

| | | | | |
|---|---|---|---|---|
| 1. import | 2. enable | 3. tractors | 4. challenge | 5. starved |
| 6. exports | 7. pests | 8. temporary | 9. luxury | 10. diameter |
| 11. expert | 12. pollution | 13. fundamental | | |

### 11b

| | | | | |
|---|---|---|---|---|
| 1. fate | 2. process | 3. bubbles | 4. hostile | 5. catalogue |
| 6. compel | 7. theft | 8. drained | 9. sites | 10. inferior |
| 11. communicate | | | | |

### 11c

| | | | | |
|---|---|---|---|---|
| 1. k | 2. e | 3. b | 4. d | 5. j |
| 6. g | 7. a | 8. i | 9. l | 10. f |
| 11. c | 12. h | | | |

### 11d

| | | | | |
|---|---|---|---|---|
| 1. instances | 2. bulk | 3. fluid | 4. topic | 5. inspecting |
| 6. switches | 7. novels | 8. fulfil | 9. revolves | 10. vital |
| 11. shrunk | 12. huge | | | |

### 11e

| | | | | |
|---|---|---|---|---|
| 1. lectures | 2. transparent | 3. captured | 4. inherent | 5. route |
| 6. irrigate | 7. defects | 8. column | 9. ratio | 10. leisure |

### 11f

| | | |
|---|---|---|
| 1. cassette tape | 2. tropical rain forests | 3. electrical circuits |
| 4. gas cylinders | 5. public transport | 6. academic websites |
| 7. mental illness | 8. television stations | 9. air fares |
| 10. career change | | |

© Peter Collin Publishing 2001. For reference see *English Dictionary for Students* (1-901659-06-2)